HERSHEY'S

Bars, Brownies & Treats

contents

BARS, BROWNIES & TREATS

22

28

58

72

classic favorites

Peanut Butter Glazed Chocolate Bars

MAKES ABOUT 40 BARS

¾	cup (1 ½ sticks) butter or margarine
½	cup HERSHEY'S Cocoa
1 ½	cups sugar
1 ½	teaspoons vanilla extract
3	eggs
1 ¼	cups all-purpose flour
¼	teaspoon baking powder
	PEANUT BUTTER FILLING AND GLAZE (recipe follows)
	CHOCOLATE DRIZZLE (recipe follows)

1 Heat oven to 350°F. Line 15½ × 10½ × 1-inch jelly-roll pan with foil; grease foil.

2 Melt butter in medium saucepan over low heat. Add cocoa; stir constantly until smooth. Remove from heat; stir in sugar and vanilla. Beat in eggs, one at a time, until well combined. Stir in flour and baking powder. Spread batter evenly in prepared pan.

3 Bake 14 to 16 minutes or until top springs back when touched lightly in center. Remove from oven; cool 2 minutes. Invert onto wire rack. Peel off foil; turn right side up on wire rack to cool completely.

4 Prepare PEANUT BUTTER FILLING AND GLAZE. Cut brownie in half; spread half of glaze evenly on one half. Top with second half; spread with remaining glaze. Cool until glaze is set. Prepare CHOCOLATE DRIZZLE; drizzle over glaze. After chocolate is set, cut into bars.

Peanut Butter Filling and Glaze:
Combine ⅓ cup sugar and ⅓ cup water in small saucepan; cook over medium heat to boiling. Remove from heat; immediately add 1⅔ cups (10-ounce package) REESE'S Peanut Butter Chips. Stir until melted. Cool slightly. Makes about 1⅓ cups glaze.

Chocolate Drizzle: Place ⅓ cup HERSHEY'S SPECIAL DARK Chocolate Chips or HERSHEY'S Semi-Sweet Chocolate Chips and 1 teaspoon shortening (do not use butter, margarine, spread or oil) in small microwave-safe bowl. Microwave at MEDIUM (50%) 30 seconds to 1 minute or until chips are melted and mixture is smooth when stirred.

Chip and Nut Blondie Cake Bars

½   cup (1 stick) butter or margarine, softened

½   cup sucralose-brown sugar blend

1   egg

1   tablespoon milk

2   teaspoons vanilla extract

1   cup all-purpose flour

½   teaspoon baking soda

¼   teaspoon salt

1⅓   cups (8-ounce package) HERSHEY'S Sugar Free Chocolate Chips, divided

½   cup coarsely chopped nuts

¼   teaspoon shortening (do not use butter, margarine, spreads or oil)

1 Heat oven to 350°F. Grease 8- or 9-inch square baking pan.

2 Beat butter and brown sugar blend in large bowl until well blended. Add egg, milk and vanilla; beat well. Stir together flour, baking soda and salt; add to butter mixture, beating until well blended.

3 Set aside 2 tablespoons chocolate chips. Stir the remaining chips and nuts into batter. Spread batter in prepared pan.

4 Bake 15 to 20 minutes or until cake begins to pull from sides of pan, toothpick inserted in center comes out clean and surface is lightly browned. (Do not overbake.) Cool completely in pan on wire rack. (As it cools the center will look underbaked.)

5 Place reserved 2 tablespoons chips and shortening in small microwave-safe bowl. Microwave at MEDIUM (50%) 30 seconds; stir. If necessary, microwave at MEDIUM an additional 10 seconds at a time, stirring after each heating, until chips are melted and smooth when stirred. Drizzle melted chocolate over surface of cake; allow to set. Cut into bars.

Chunky Macadamia Bars

MAKES 24 BARS

¾   cup (1 ½ sticks) butter or margarine, softened

1   cup packed light brown sugar

½   cup granulated sugar

1   egg

1   teaspoon vanilla extract

2 ¼   cups all-purpose flour

1   teaspoon baking soda

1 ¾   cups (10-ounce package) HERSHEY'S MINI KISSESBRAND Milk Chocolates, divided

¾   cup MAUNA LOA Macadamia Baking Pieces

VANILLA GLAZE (recipe follows)

1 Heat oven to 375°F.

2 Beat butter, brown sugar and granulated sugar in large bowl until fluffy. Add egg and vanilla; beat well. Add flour and baking soda; blend well. Stir in 1 cup chocolate pieces and nuts; press into ungreased 13×9×2-inch baking pan. Sprinkle with remaining ¾ cup chocolates.

3 Bake 22 to 25 minutes or until golden brown. Cool completely in pan on wire rack. Drizzle VANILLA GLAZE over top; allow to set. Cut into bars.

Vanilla Glaze: Combine 1 cup powdered sugar, 2 tablespoons milk and ½ teaspoon vanilla extract in small bowl; stir until smooth. Makes ⅓ cup glaze.

Perfectly Peppermint Brownies

MAKES ABOUT 3 DOZEN BROWNIES

¾	cup HERSHEY'S Cocoa
½	teaspoon baking soda
⅔	cup butter or margarine, melted and divided
½	cup boiling water
2	cups sugar
2	eggs
1⅓	cups all-purpose flour
1	teaspoon vanilla extract
¼	teaspoon salt
16	to 17 small (1½-inch) YORK Peppermint Patties, unwrapped and coarsely chopped

1 Heat oven to 350°F. Grease 13×9×2-inch baking pan.

2 Stir together cocoa and baking soda in large bowl; stir in ⅓ cup butter. Add boiling water; stir until mixture thickens. Stir in sugar, eggs and remaining ⅓ cup butter; stir until smooth. Add flour, vanilla and salt; blend completely. Stir in peppermint pattie pieces. Spread in prepared pan.

3 Bake 35 to 40 minutes or until brownies begin to pull away from sides of pan. Cool completely in pan on wire rack. Cut into bars.

Double Peanut Butter Paisley Brownies

MAKES ABOUT 36 BROWNIES

- ½ cup (1 stick) butter or margarine, softened
- ¼ cup REESE'S Creamy Peanut Butter
- 1 cup granulated sugar
- 1 cup packed light brown sugar
- 3 eggs
- 1 teaspoon vanilla extract
- 2 cups all-purpose flour
- 2 teaspoons baking powder
- ¼ teaspoon salt
- 1⅔ cups (10-ounce package) REESE'S Peanut Butter Chips
- ½ cup HERSHEY'S Syrup or HERSHEY'S SPECIAL DARK Syrup

1 Heat oven to 350°F. Grease 13×9×2-inch baking pan.

2 Beat butter and peanut butter in large bowl. Add granulated sugar and brown sugar; beat well. Add eggs, one at a time, beating well after each addition. Blend in vanilla.

3 Stir together flour, baking powder and salt; mix into peanut butter mixture, blending well. Stir in peanut butter chips. Spread half of batter in prepared pan; spoon syrup over top. Carefully top with remaining batter; swirl with metal spatula or knife for marbled effect.

4 Bake 35 to 40 minutes or until lightly browned. Cool completely in pan on wire rack. Cut into squares.

Brownies in a Jar

MAKES 1 JAR MIX

1	cup all-purpose flour
½	teaspoon baking powder
¼	teaspoon salt
1½	cups sugar
⅓	cup HERSHEY'S SPECIAL DARK Cocoa
1	cup REESE'S Peanut Butter Chips or HERSHEY'S Premier White Chips
½	cup HERSHEY'S Mini Chips Semi-Sweet Chocolate
	BAKING INSTRUCTIONS (recipe follows)

1 Stir together flour, baking powder and salt in a small bowl.

2 Layer the ingredients in a clean 1-quart glass canister or jar in the following order (from bottom to top): sugar, cocoa, flour mixture, peanut butter chips and small chocolate chips. Tap jar gently on the counter to settle each layer before adding the next one. Close jar. Attach card with BAKING INSTRUCTIONS.

Baking Instructions: Heat oven to 350°F. Grease and flour an 8-inch square baking pan. Combine ½ cup (1 stick) melted and cooled butter and 2 slightly beaten eggs in a large bowl. Gently stir in jar contents. Spread in prepared pan. Bake for 35 minutes. Cool in pan. Cut into bars.

MAKES 16 BROWNIES

Rocky Road Tasty Team Treats

MAKES ABOUT 36 BARS

1 ½   cups finely crushed thin pretzels or pretzel sticks

¾   cup (1 ½ sticks) butter or margarine, melted

1   can (14 ounces) sweetened condensed milk (not evaporated milk)

1 ¾   cups (10-ounce package) HERSHEY'S MINI KISSES BRAND Milk Chocolates

3   cups miniature marshmallows

1 ⅓   cups coarsely chopped pecans or pecan pieces

1 Heat oven to 350°F. Grease bottom and sides of 13×9×2-inch baking pan.

2 Combine pretzels and melted butter in small bowl; press evenly onto bottom of prepared pan. Spread sweetened condensed milk evenly over pretzel layer; layer evenly with chocolates, marshmallows and pecans, in order. Press down firmly on pecans.

3 Bake 20 to 25 minutes or until lightly browned. Cool completely in pan on wire rack. Cut into bars.

All American HEATH Brownies

MAKES 16 BROWNIES

⅓	cup butter or margarine
3	sections (½ ounce each) HERSHEY'S Unsweetened Chocolate Baking Bar
1	cup sugar
2	eggs
1	teaspoon vanilla extract
1	cup all-purpose flour
½	teaspoon baking powder
¼	teaspoon salt
1⅓	cups (8-ounce package) HEATH Milk Chocolate Toffee Bits

1 Heat oven to 350°F. Grease bottom of 8-inch square baking pan.

2 Melt butter and chocolate in medium saucepan over low heat, stirring occasionally. Stir in sugar. Add eggs, one at a time, beating after each addition. Stir in vanilla. Combine flour, baking powder and salt; add to chocolate mixture, stirring until well blended. Spread batter in prepared pan.

3 Bake 20 minutes or until brownie begins to pull away from sides of pan. Remove from oven; sprinkle with toffee bits. Cover tightly with foil and cool completely on wire rack. Remove foil; cut into squares.

Best Fudgey Pecan Brownies

½   cup (1 stick) butter or margarine, melted

1   cup sugar

1   teaspoon vanilla extract

2   eggs

½   cup all-purpose flour

⅓   cup HERSHEY'S Cocoa

¼   teaspoon baking powder

¼   teaspoon salt

½   cup coarsely chopped pecans

CHOCOLATE PECAN FROSTING (recipe follows)

Pecan halves

1 Heat oven to 350°F. Lightly grease 8- or 9-inch square baking pan.

2 Beat butter, sugar and vanilla with spoon in large bowl. Add eggs; beat well. Stir together flour, cocoa, baking powder and salt; gradually add to egg mixture, beating until well blended. Stir in chopped pecans. Spread in prepared pan.

3 Bake 20 to 25 minutes or until brownies begin to pull away from sides of pan. Meanwhile, prepare CHOCOLATE PECAN FROSTING. Spread warm frosting over warm brownies. Garnish with pecan halves. Cool completely; cut into squares.

Chocolate Pecan Frosting

1⅓   cups powdered sugar

2   tablespoons HERSHEY'S Cocoa

3   tablespoons butter or margarine

2   tablespoons milk

¼   teaspoon vanilla extract

¼   cup chopped pecans

1 Stir together powdered sugar and cocoa in medium bowl.

2 Heat butter and milk in small saucepan over low heat until butter is melted. Gradually beat into cocoa mixture, beating until smooth. Stir in vanilla and pecans.

MAKES ABOUT 1 CUP FROSTING

Double Chip Brownies

MAKES ABOUT 36 BROWNIES

¾	cup HERSHEY'S Cocoa
½	teaspoon baking soda
⅔	cup butter or margarine, melted and divided
½	cup boiling water
2	cups sugar
2	eggs
1⅓	cups all-purpose flour
1	teaspoon vanilla extract
¼	teaspoon salt
1	cup HERSHEY'S Milk Chocolate Chips
1	cup REESE'S Peanut Butter Chips

1 Heat oven to 350°F. Grease 13×9×2-inch baking pan.

2 Stir together cocoa and baking soda in large bowl; stir in ⅓ cup melted butter. Add boiling water; stir until mixture thickens. Stir in sugar, eggs and remaining ⅓ cup melted butter; stir until smooth. Add flour, vanilla and salt; blend thoroughly. Stir in milk chocolate chips and peanut butter chips. Spread in prepared pan.

3 Bake 35 to 40 minutes or until brownies begin to pull away from sides of pan. Cool completely in pan on wire rack. Cut into squares.

Chocolate Cranberry Bars

MAKES 36 BARS

2	cups vanilla wafer crumbs (about 60 wafers, crushed)
½	cup HERSHEY'S Cocoa
3	tablespoons sugar
⅔	cup cold butter, cut into pieces
1	can (14 ounces) sweetened condensed milk (not evaporated milk)
1	cup REESE'S Peanut Butter Chips
1⅓	cups (6-ounce package) sweetened dried cranberries or 1⅓ cups raisins
1	cup coarsely chopped walnuts

1 Heat oven to 350°F.

2 Stir together vanilla wafer crumbs, cocoa and sugar in medium bowl; cut in butter until crumbly. Press mixture evenly on bottom and ½ inch up sides of 13×9×2-inch baking pan. Pour sweetened condensed milk evenly over crumb mixture; sprinkle evenly with peanut butter chips and dried cranberries. Sprinkle nuts on top; press down firmly.

3 Bake 25 to 30 minutes or until lightly browned. Cool completely in pan on wire rack. Cover with foil; let stand several hours before cutting into bars and serving.

English Toffee Bars

MAKES ABOUT 36 BARS

- **2** cups all-purpose flour
- **1** cup packed light brown sugar
- **½** cup (1 stick) cold butter
- **1** cup pecan halves
- **TOFFEE TOPPING (recipe follows)**
- **1** cup HERSHEY'S Milk Chocolate Chips

1 Heat oven to 350°F.

2 Combine flour and brown sugar in large bowl. With pastry blender or fork, cut in butter until fine crumbs form (a few large crumbs may remain). Press mixture onto bottom of ungreased 13×9×2-inch baking pan. Sprinkle pecans over crust. Prepare TOFFEE TOPPING; drizzle evenly over pecans and crust.

3 Bake 20 to 22 minutes or until topping is bubbly and golden; remove from oven. Immediately sprinkle milk chocolate chips evenly over top; press gently onto surface. Cool completely in pan on wire rack. Cut into bars.

Toffee Topping: Combine ⅔ cup butter and ⅓ cup packed light brown sugar in small saucepan; cook over medium heat, stirring constantly, until mixture comes to a boil. Continue boiling, stirring constantly, 30 seconds. Use immediately.

HERSHEY'S Best Brownies

MAKES ABOUT 36 BROWNIES

- **1** cup (2 sticks) butter or margarine
- **2** cups sugar
- **2** teaspoons vanilla extract
- **4** eggs
- **¾** cup HERSHEY'S Cocoa or HERSHEY'S SPECIAL DARK Cocoa
- **1** cup all-purpose flour
- **½** teaspoon baking powder
- **¼** teaspoon salt
- **1** cup chopped nuts (optional)

1 Heat oven to 350°F. Grease 13×9×2-inch baking pan.

2 Place butter in large microwave-safe bowl. Microwave at MEDIUM (50%) 2 to 2½ minutes or until melted. Stir in sugar and vanilla. Add eggs, one at a time, beating well with spoon after each addition. Add cocoa; beat until well blended. Add flour, baking powder and salt; beat well. Stir in nuts, if desired. Pour batter into prepared pan.

3 Bake 30 to 35 minutes or until brownies begin to pull away from sides of pan. Cool completely in pan on wire rack. Frost, if desired. Cut into bars.

Peppermint Pattie Fudge Bars

MAKES 36 BARS

16	or 17 small (1½-inch) YORK Peppermint Patties, divided
1½	cups vanilla wafer crumbs (about 45 wafers, crushed)
½	cup HERSHEY'S SPECIAL DARK Cocoa, divided
½	cup powdered sugar
¼	cup (½ stick) butter or margarine, melted
1	can (14 ounces) sweetened condensed milk (not evaporated milk)
¼	cup all-purpose flour
1	egg
1	teaspoon vanilla extract
½	teaspoon baking powder
	Additional powdered sugar
½	teaspoon water

1 Heat oven to 350°F. Unwrap and coarsely chop peppermint patties; set aside. Stir together cookie crumbs, ¼ cup cocoa, ½ cup powdered sugar and melted butter. Press firmly on bottom of ungreased 13×9×2-inch baking pan.

2 Beat sweetened condensed milk, flour, remaining ¼ cup cocoa, egg, vanilla and baking powder in large bowl until well blended. Spread evenly over prepared crust. Set aside 2 tablespoons peppermint pattie pieces; sprinkle remaining pieces over filling.

3 Bake 18 to 23 minutes or until set. Cool completely in pan on wire rack. Sprinkle cooled bars with additional powdered sugar.

4 Place reserved peppermint patties and water in small microwave-safe bowl. Microwave at MEDIUM (50%) 30 seconds; stir. If necessary, microwave an additional 10 seconds at a time, stirring after each heating, until patties are melted and smooth when stirred. Immediately drizzle over bars. Allow drizzle to set. Cut into bars.

Thick and Fudgey Brownies with HERSHEY'S MINI KISSES Milk Chocolates

MAKES 24 BROWNIES

2¼	cups all-purpose flour
⅔	cup HERSHEY'S Cocoa
1	teaspoon baking powder
1	teaspoon salt
¾	cup (1½ sticks) butter or margarine, melted
2½	cups sugar
2	teaspoons vanilla extract
4	eggs
1¾	cups (10-ounce package) HERSHEY'S MINI KISSESBRAND Milk Chocolates

1 Heat oven to 350°F (325°F for glass baking dish). Grease 13×9×2-inch baking pan.

2 Stir together flour, cocoa, baking powder and salt. With spoon or whisk, stir together butter, sugar and vanilla in large bowl. Add eggs; stir until well blended. Stir in flour mixture, blending well. Stir in chocolate pieces. Spread batter in prepared pan.

3 Bake 30 to 35 minutes or until brownies begin to pull away from sides of pan. Cool completely in pan on wire rack; cut into 2-inch squares.

MINI KISSES Blondies

MAKES ABOUT 36 BARS

½	cup (1 stick) butter or margarine, softened
1⅓	cups packed light brown sugar
2	eggs
2	teaspoons vanilla extract
¼	teaspoon salt
2	cups all-purpose flour
1½	teaspoons baking powder
1¾	cups (10-ounce package) HERSHEY'S MINI KISSESBRAND Milk Chocolates
½	cup chopped nuts

1 Heat oven to 350°F. Lightly grease 13×9×2-inch baking pan.

2 Beat butter and brown sugar in large bowl until fluffy. Add eggs, vanilla and salt; beat until blended. Add flour and baking powder; beat just until blended. Stir in chocolate pieces. Spread batter in prepared pan. Sprinkle nuts over top.

3 Bake 28 to 30 minutes or until set and golden brown. Cool completely in pan on wire rack. Cut into bars.

Rocky Road Brownies

MAKES ABOUT 20 BROWNIES

1 ¼   cups miniature marshmallows

1   cup HERSHEY'S SPECIAL DARK Chocolate Chips or HERSHEY'S Semi-Sweet Chocolate Chips

½   cup chopped nuts

½   cup (1 stick) butter or margarine

1   cup sugar

2   eggs

1   teaspoon vanilla extract

½   cup all-purpose flour

⅓   cup HERSHEY'S Cocoa

½   teaspoon baking powder

½   teaspoon salt

1 Heat oven to 350°F. Grease 9-inch square baking pan.

2 Stir together marshmallows, chocolate chips and nuts; set aside. Place butter in large microwave-safe bowl. Microwave at MEDIUM (50%) 1 to 1 ½ minutes or until melted. Add sugar, eggs and vanilla, beating with spoon until well blended. Add flour, cocoa, baking powder and salt; blend well. Spread batter in prepared pan.

3 Bake 22 minutes. Sprinkle chocolate chip mixture over top. Continue baking 5 minutes or until marshmallows have softened and puffed slightly. Cool completely in pan on wire rack. With wet knife, cut into squares.

Simply Special Brownies

½   **cup (1 stick) butter or margarine**

1   **package (4 ounces) HERSHEY'S Semi-Sweet Chocolate Baking Bar, broken into pieces**

2   **eggs**

1   **teaspoon vanilla extract**

¾   **teaspoon powdered instant coffee**

⅔   **cup sugar**

½   **cup all-purpose flour**

¼   **teaspoon baking soda**

¼   **teaspoon salt**

½   **cup coarsely chopped nuts (optional)**

1 Heat oven to 350°F. Grease 9-inch square baking pan.

2 Place butter and chocolate in medium microwave-safe bowl. Microwave at MEDIUM (50%) 1 minute; stir. If necessary, microwave an additional 15 seconds at a time, stirring after each heating, until chocolate is melted and mixture is smooth when stirred. Add eggs, vanilla and instant coffee, stirring until well blended. Stir in sugar, flour, baking soda and salt; blend completely. Stir in nuts, if desired. Spread batter in prepared pan.

3 Bake 25 to 30 minutes or until wooden pick inserted in center comes out almost clean. Cool completely in pan on wire rack. Cut into bars.

HERSHEY'S Brownies
with Peanut Butter Frosting

MAKES ABOUT 16 BROWNIES

½   cup (1 stick) butter or margarine

4   sections (½ ounce each) **HERSHEY'S Unsweetened Chocolate Baking Bar**, broken into pieces

1   cup sugar

2   eggs

1   teaspoon vanilla extract

½   cup all-purpose flour

¼   teaspoon baking powder

¼   teaspoon salt

½   cup chopped nuts

PEANUT BUTTER FROSTING (recipe follows, optional)

1 Heat oven to 350°F. Grease 8-inch square baking pan.

2 Melt butter and chocolate in medium saucepan over low heat. Remove from heat; stir in sugar. Beat in eggs and vanilla with wooden spoon. Stir together flour, baking powder and salt. Add to chocolate mixture, blending well. Stir in nuts. Pour batter into prepared pan.

3 Bake 30 to 35 minutes or until brownies begin to pull away from sides of pan. Cool completely in pan on wire rack. Frost with PEANUT BUTTER FROSTING, if desired. Cut into squares.

Peanut Butter Frosting

1   cup powdered sugar

¼   cup **REESE'S Creamy Peanut Butter**

2   tablespoons milk

½   teaspoon vanilla extract

Combine all ingredients in small bowl; beat until smooth. If necessary add additional milk, ½ teaspoon at a time, until of desired consistency.

MAKES ABOUT ¾ CUP FROSTING

indulgent goodies

Chocolate Almond Macaroon Bars

MAKES ABOUT 36 BARS

- 2 cups chocolate wafer cookie crumbs
- 6 tablespoons butter or margarine, melted
- 6 tablespoons powdered sugar
- 1 can (14 ounces) sweetened condensed milk (not evaporated milk)
- 3¾ cups MOUNDS Sweetened Coconut Flakes
- 1 cup sliced almonds, toasted* (optional)
- 1 cup HERSHEY'S SPECIAL DARK Chocolate Chips or HERSHEY'S Semi-Sweet Chocolate Chips
- ¼ cup whipping cream
- ½ cup HERSHEY'S Premier White Chips

To toast almonds: Heat oven to 350°F. Spread almonds evenly on shallow baking sheet. Bake 5 to 8 minutes or until lightly browned.

1 Heat oven to 350°F. Grease 13×9×2-inch baking pan.

2 Combine crumbs, melted butter and powdered sugar in large bowl. Firmly press crumb mixture on bottom of prepared pan. Stir together sweetened condensed milk, coconut and almonds in large bowl, mixing well. Carefully drop mixture by spoonfuls over crust; spread evenly.

3 Bake 20 to 25 minutes or until coconut edges just begin to brown. Cool.

4 Place chocolate chips and whipping cream in medium microwave-safe bowl. Microwave at MEDIUM (50%) 1 minute; stir. If necessary, microwave at MEDIUM an additional 15 seconds at a time, stirring after each heating, until chips are melted and mixture is smooth when stirred. Cool until slightly thickened; spread over cooled bars. Sprinkle top with white chips. Cover; refrigerate several hours or until thoroughly chilled. Cut into bars. Refrigerate leftovers.

Peanut Butter and Milk Chocolate Chip Tassies

- ¾ cup (1½ sticks) butter, softened
- 1 package (3 ounces) cream cheese, softened
- 1½ cups all-purpose flour
- ¾ cup sugar, divided
- 1 egg, slightly beaten
- 2 tablespoons butter or margarine, melted
- ¼ teaspoon lemon juice
- ¼ teaspoon vanilla extract
- 1 cup HERSHEY'S Milk Chocolate Chips
- 1 cup REESE'S Peanut Butter Chips
- 2 teaspoons shortening (do not use butter, margarine, spread or oil)

1 Beat ¾ cup butter and cream cheese in medium bowl; add flour and ¼ cup sugar, beating until well blended. Cover; refrigerate about one hour or until dough is firm. Shape dough into 1-inch balls; press balls onto bottoms and up sides of about 36 small muffin cups (1¾ inches in diameter).

2 Heat oven to 350°F. Combine egg, remaining ½ cup sugar, melted butter, lemon juice and vanilla in small bowl; stir until smooth. Stir together milk chocolate chips and peanut butter chips. Set aside ⅓ cup chip mixture; add remaining chips to egg mixture. Evenly fill muffin cups with egg mixture.

3 Bake 20 to 25 minutes or until filling is set and lightly browned. Cool completely; remove from pan to wire rack.

4 Combine remaining ⅓ cup chip mixture and shortening in small microwave-safe bowl. Microwave at MEDIUM (50%) 30 seconds; stir. If necessary, microwave additional 10 seconds at a time, stirring after each heating, until chips are melted and mixture is smooth when stirred. Drizzle over tops of tassies.

Layered Cookie Bars

MAKES ABOUT 36 BARS

¾ cup (1½ sticks) butter or margarine

1¾ cups vanilla wafer crumbs (about 50 wafers, crushed)

6 tablespoons HERSHEY'S Cocoa

¼ cup sugar

1 can (14 ounces) sweetened condensed milk (not evaporated milk)

1 cup HERSHEY'S SPECIAL DARK Chocolate Chips or HERSHEY'S Semi-Sweet Chocolate Chips

¾ cup HEATH BITS 'O BRICKLE Toffee Bits

1 cup chopped walnuts

1 Heat oven to 350°F. Melt butter in 13×9×2-inch baking pan in oven. Combine crumbs, cocoa and sugar; sprinkle over butter.

2 Pour sweetened condensed milk evenly on top of crumbs. Top with chocolate chips and toffee bits, then nuts; press down firmly.

3 Bake 25 to 30 minutes or until lightly browned. Cool completely in pan on wire rack. Chill, if desired. Cut into bars. Store covered at room temperature.

Chippy Chewy Bars

MAKES ABOUT 48 BARS

½ cup (1 stick) butter or margarine

1½ cups graham cracker crumbs

1⅔ cups (10-ounce package) REESE'S Peanut Butter Chips

1½ cups MOUNDS Sweetened Coconut Flakes

1 can (14 ounces) sweetened condensed milk (not evaporated milk)

½ cup HERSHEY'S SPECIAL DARK Chocolate Chips, HERSHEY'S Semi-Sweet Chocolate Chips or HERSHEY'S Mini Chips Semi-Sweet Chocolate

¾ teaspoon shortening (do not use butter, margarine, spread or oil)

1 Heat oven to 350°F. Place butter in 13×9×2-inch baking pan. Heat in oven until melted; remove pan from oven. Sprinkle graham cracker crumbs evenly over butter; press down with fork.

2 Sprinkle peanut butter chips over crumbs; sprinkle coconut over chips. Drizzle sweetened condensed milk evenly over top.

3 Bake 20 minutes or until lightly browned.

4 Place chocolate chips and shortening in small microwave-safe bowl. Microwave at MEDIUM (50%) 30 seconds; stir. If necessary, microwave at MEDIUM an additional 10 seconds at a time, stirring after each heating, just until chips are melted when stirred. Drizzle evenly over top of baked mixture. Cool completely. Cut into bars.

White Chip Lemon Streusel Bars

- 1 can (14 ounces) sweetened condensed milk (not evaporated milk)
- ½ cup lemon juice
- 1 teaspoon freshly grated lemon peel
- 2 cups (12-ounce package) HERSHEY'S Premier White Chips, divided
- ⅔ cup butter or margarine, softened
- 1 cup packed light brown sugar
- 1½ cups all-purpose flour
- 1½ cups regular rolled or quick-cooking oats
- ¾ cup toasted pecan pieces*
- 1 teaspoon baking powder
- ½ teaspoon salt
- 1 egg
- ½ teaspoon shortening

*To toast pecans: Heat oven to 350°F. Spread pecans in thin layer in shallow baking pan. Bake, stirring occasionally, 7 to 8 minutes or until golden brown; cool.

1 Heat oven to 350°F. Lightly grease 13×9×2-inch baking pan. Combine sweetened condensed milk, lemon juice and lemon peel in medium bowl; set aside. Measure out ¼ cup and ⅓ cup white chips; set aside. Add remaining white chips to lemon mixture.

2 Beat butter and brown sugar with electric mixer on medium speed in large bowl until well blended. Stir together flour, oats, pecans, baking powder and salt; add to butter mixture, blending well. Set aside 1⅔ cups oats mixture. Add egg to remaining oats mixture, blending until crumbly; press onto bottom of prepared pan. Gently spoon lemon mixture on top, spreading evenly. Add reserved ⅓ cup white chips to reserved oats mixture. Sprinkle over lemon layer, pressing down lightly.

3 Bake 20 to 25 minutes or until lightly browned. Cool in pan on wire rack. Place remaining ¼ cup white chips and shortening in small microwave-safe bowl. Microwave at MEDIUM (50%) 30 seconds or until chips are melted and mixture is smooth when stirred. Drizzle over baked bars. Allow drizzle to set; cut into bars.

Cranberry Orange Ricotta Cheese Brownies

MAKES ABOUT 16 BROWNIES

½ **cup (1 stick) butter or margarine, melted**

¾ **cup sugar**

1 **teaspoon vanilla extract**

2 **eggs**

¾ **cup all-purpose flour**

½ **cup HERSHEY'S Cocoa**

½ **teaspoon baking powder**

½ **teaspoon salt**

CHEESE FILLING (recipe follows)

1 Heat oven to 350°F. Grease 9-inch square baking pan.

2 Stir together butter, sugar and vanilla in medium bowl; add eggs, beating well. Stir together flour, cocoa, baking powder and salt; add to butter mixture, mixing thoroughly. Spread half of chocolate batter in prepared pan. Spread CHEESE FILLING over top. Drop remaining chocolate batter by teaspoonfuls onto CHEESE FILLING.

3 Bake 40 to 45 minutes or until wooden pick inserted in center comes out clean. Cool completely in pan on wire rack. Cut into squares. Refrigerate leftover brownies.

Cheese Filling

1 **cup ricotta cheese**

¼ **cup sugar**

3 **tablespoons whole-berry cranberry sauce**

2 **tablespoons cornstarch**

1 **egg**

¼ **to ½ teaspoon freshly grated orange peel**

4 **drops red food color (optional)**

Beat ricotta cheese, sugar, cranberry sauce, cornstarch and egg in small bowl until smooth. Stir in orange peel and food color, if desired.

Peanut Butter Fudge Brownie Bars

MAKES 36 BARS

1	cup (2 sticks) butter or margarine, melted
1½	cups sugar
2	eggs
1	teaspoon vanilla extract
1¼	cups all-purpose flour
⅔	cup HERSHEY'S Cocoa
¼	cup milk
1¼	cups chopped pecans or walnuts, divided
½	cup (1 stick) butter or margarine
1⅔	cups (10-ounce package) REESE'S Peanut Butter Chips
1	can (14 ounces) sweetened condensed milk (not evaporated milk)
¼	cup HERSHEY'S SPECIAL DARK Chocolate Chips or HERSHEY'S Semi-Sweet Chocolate Chips

1 Heat oven to 350°F. Grease 13×9×2-inch baking pan.

2 Beat melted butter, sugar, eggs and vanilla in large bowl with electric mixer on medium speed until well blended. Add flour, cocoa and milk; beat until blended. Stir in 1 cup nuts. Spread in prepared pan.

3 Bake 25 to 30 minutes or just until edges begin to pull away from sides of pan. Cool completely in pan on wire rack.

4 Melt ½ cup butter and peanut butter chips in medium saucepan over low heat, stirring constantly. Add sweetened condensed milk, stirring until smooth; pour over baked layer.

5 Place chocolate chips in small microwave-safe bowl. Microwave at MEDIUM (50%) 45 seconds or just until chips are melted when stirred. Drizzle bars with melted chocolate; sprinkle with remaining ¼ cup nuts. Refrigerate 1 hour or until firm. Cut into bars. Cover; refrigerate leftover bars.

Marbled Cheesecake Bars

MAKES 24 TO 36 BARS

CHOCOLATE CRUST (recipe follows)

3 packages (8 ounces each) cream cheese, softened

1 can (14 ounces) sweetened condensed milk (not evaporated milk)

3 eggs

2 teaspoons vanilla extract

4 sections (½ ounce each) HERSHEY'S Unsweetened Chocolate Baking Bar, melted

1 Prepare CHOCOLATE CRUST. Heat oven to 300°F.

2 Beat cream cheese in large bowl until fluffy. Gradually add sweetened condensed milk, beating until smooth. Add eggs and vanilla; mix well.

3 Pour half of batter evenly over prepared crust. Stir melted chocolate into remaining batter; drop by spoonfuls over vanilla batter. With metal spatula or knife, swirl gently through batter to marble.

4 Bake 45 to 50 minutes or until set. Cool in pan on wire rack. Refrigerate several hours until chilled. Cut into bars. Cover; store leftover bars in refrigerator.

Chocolate Crust: Stir together 2 cups vanilla wafer crumbs (about 60 wafers, crushed), ⅓ cup HERSHEY'S Cocoa and ½ cup powdered sugar. Stir in ½ cup (1 stick) melted butter or margarine until well blended. Press mixture firmly onto bottom of ungreased 13×9×2-inch baking pan.

S'mores Sandwich Bar Cookies

MAKES 16 BARS

- ½ cup (1 stick) butter or margarine, softened
- ¾ cup sugar
- 1 egg
- 1 teaspoon vanilla extract
- 1⅓ cups all-purpose flour
- ¾ cup graham cracker crumbs
- 1 teaspoon baking powder
- ¼ teaspoon salt
- 5 HERSHEY'S Milk Chocolate Bars (1.55 ounces each), broken in pieces
- 3 cups miniature marshmallows

1 Heat oven to 350°F. Grease 8-inch square baking pan.

2 Beat butter and sugar in large bowl until well blended. Add egg and vanilla; beat well. Stir together flour, graham cracker crumbs, baking powder and salt; add to butter mixture, beating until blended. Press half of dough into prepared pan. Bake 15 minutes.

3 Sprinkle chocolate bar sections, marshmallows and bits of remaining dough over baked layer. Bake 10 to 15 minutes or just until lightly browned. Cool completely in pan on wire rack. Cut into bars.

Peanut Butter Chip Fruit Bars

MAKES 24 BARS

1½ cups REESE'S Peanut Butter Chips, divided

1 package (8 ounces) cream cheese, softened

1 cup packed light brown sugar

1 egg

1 teaspoon vanilla extract

1 cup all-purpose flour

½ teaspoon baking soda

¼ teaspoon salt

½ cup quick-cooking oats

1 cup chopped dried mixed fruit or dried fruit bits

1 cup powdered sugar

2 tablespoons orange juice

¼ teaspoon freshly grated orange peel (optional)

1 Heat oven to 350°F. Grease 13×9×2-inch baking pan.

2 Place 1 cup peanut butter chips in microwave-safe bowl. Microwave at MEDIUM (50%) 1 minute; stir. If necessary, microwave an additional 15 seconds at a time, stirring after each heating, until chips are melted and smooth when stirred. Beat melted peanut butter chips and cream cheese in large bowl until well blended. Add brown sugar, egg and vanilla; blend well. Stir together flour, baking soda and salt; add to cream cheese mixture, blending well. Stir in oats, remaining ½ cup peanut butter chips and dried fruit.

3 Spread batter in prepared pan. Bake 20 to 25 minutes or until golden brown. Cool in pan on wire rack.

4 Meanwhile, stir together powdered sugar, orange juice and grated orange peel in small mixing bowl; blend until smooth. (Add additional orange juice, a teaspoonful at a time, if glaze is too thick.) Pour over bars and cool completely. Cut into bars.

Chocolate Orange Cheesecake Bars

MAKES 24 BARS

- **1** cup all-purpose flour
- **½** cup packed light brown sugar
- **¼** teaspoon ground cinnamon (optional)
- **⅓** cup shortening
- **½** cup chopped pecans
- **CHOCOLATE ORANGE FILLING (recipe follows)**
- Pecan halves (optional)

1 Heat oven to 350°F.

2 Stir together flour, brown sugar and cinnamon, if desired, in large bowl. Cut shortening into flour mixture with pastry blender or two knives until mixture resembles coarse crumbs. Stir in chopped pecans. Reserve ¾ cup flour mixture. Press remaining mixture firmly onto bottom of ungreased 9-inch square baking pan. Bake 10 minutes or until lightly browned.

3 Spread CHOCOLATE ORANGE FILLING over warm crust. Sprinkle with reserved flour mixture. Press pecan halves lightly onto top, if desired. Return to oven. Bake 25 to 30 minutes or until lightly browned. Cool; cut into bars. Cover; refrigerate leftover bars.

Chocolate Orange Filling

- **1** package (8 ounces) cream cheese, softened
- **⅔** cup sugar
- **⅓** cup HERSHEY'S Cocoa
- **¼** cup milk
- **1** egg
- **1** teaspoon vanilla extract
- **¼** teaspoon freshly grated orange peel

Beat cream cheese and sugar with electric mixer on medium speed in medium bowl until fluffy. Add cocoa, milk, egg, vanilla and orange peel; beat until smooth.

Peanut Butter Polka Dot Bars

¾	cup butter or margarine, softened
¾	cup REESE'S Creamy Peanut Butter
2	cups light brown sugar, packed
2	eggs
1	teaspoon vanilla extract
2½	cups quick-cooking rolled oats
2½	cups all-purpose flour
1	teaspoon baking soda
½	teaspoon salt
	CHOCOLATE FILLING (recipe follows)
1⅓	cups (10-ounce package) REESE'S MINI PIECES Candies

1 Heat oven to 350°F. Beat butter, peanut butter and brown sugar until well blended. Add eggs and vanilla; beat thoroughly.

2 Stir together oats, flour, baking soda and salt; gradually add to butter mixture. (Dough will be thick.) Remove 2 cups dough; set aside. Press remaining dough onto bottom of 13×9×2-inch baking pan.

3 Prepare CHOCOLATE FILLING. Spread filling evenly over dough. Sprinkle candy pieces evenly over filling. Crumble reserved dough evenly over filling.

4 Bake 25 minutes or until top is golden brown. (Chocolate will be soft.) Cool completely in pan on wire rack; cut into bars.

Chocolate Filling: Melt ½ cup (1 stick) butter or margarine in saucepan over low heat. Stir in ⅔ cup HERSHEY'S Cocoa and ⅓ cup sugar. Add 1 can (14 ounces) sweetened condensed milk; cook, stirring constantly, until smooth and thick. Remove from heat; stir in 1½ teaspoons vanilla extract.

Layered Apricot Snacking Bars

- 2 cups (12-ounce package) HERSHEY'S Premier White Chips, divided
- 1 package (6 ounces) dried apricots, cut into ¼-inch pieces
- 1 cup boiling water
- ½ cup (1 stick) margarine, softened
- ⅓ cup granulated sugar
- ¼ cup packed light brown sugar
- 1 egg
- 1 teaspoon vanilla extract
- 1 cup plus 2 tablespoons all-purpose flour, divided
- ¼ teaspoon baking soda
- ¼ teaspoon salt
- ½ cup wheat germ
- 2 tablespoons honey
- 1 egg white
- ½ teaspoon shortening

1 Heat oven to 350°F.

2 Measure ⅓ cup white chips for glaze; set aside. Stir together apricots and water in small bowl; cover. Let stand 5 minutes; drain. Meanwhile, in large bowl, beat margarine, granulated sugar, brown sugar, egg and vanilla until well blended.

3 Stir together 1 cup flour, baking soda and salt; gradually add to margarine mixture, beating until well blended. Stir in remaining 1⅔ cups white chips; press mixture onto bottom of ungreased 8-inch square baking pan. Spread softened apricots over cookie base. Stir together wheat germ, remaining 2 tablespoons flour, honey and egg white until blended; crumble over apricots.

4 Bake 30 to 35 minutes or until wheat germ and edges are lightly browned. Cool completely in pan on wire rack.

5 Stir together reserved white chips and shortening in small microwave-safe bowl. Microwave at MEDIUM (50%) 30 seconds; stir. If necessary, microwave at MEDIUM an additional 10 seconds at a time, stirring after each heating, just until chips are melted when stirred. Using tines of fork, drizzle mixture over top; let stand until glaze is firm. Cut into bars.

Chocolate Chip Candy Cookie Bars

MAKES ABOUT 48 BARS

- 1⅔ cups all-purpose flour
- 2 tablespoons plus 1½ cups sugar, divided
- ¾ teaspoon baking powder
- 1 cup (2 sticks) cold butter or margarine, divided
- 1 egg, slightly beaten
- ½ cup plus 2 tablespoons (5-ounce can) evaporated milk, divided
- 2 cups (12-ounce package) HERSHEY'S SPECIAL DARK Chocolate Chips or HERSHEY'S Semi-Sweet Chocolate Chips, divided
- ½ cup light corn syrup
- 1½ cups sliced almonds

1 Heat oven to 375°F.

2 Stir together flour, 2 tablespoons sugar and baking powder in medium bowl; using pastry blender, cut in ½ cup butter until mixture forms coarse crumbs. Stir in egg and 2 tablespoons evaporated milk; stir until mixture holds together in ball shape. Press onto bottom and ¼ inch up sides of 15½ × 10½ × 1-inch jelly-roll pan.

3 Bake 8 to 10 minutes or until lightly browned; remove from oven, leaving oven on. Sprinkle 1½ cups chocolate chips evenly over crust; do not disturb chips.

4 Place remaining 1½ cups sugar, remaining ½ cup butter, remaining ½ cup evaporated milk and corn syrup in 3-quart saucepan. Cook over medium heat, stirring constantly, until mixture boils; stir in almonds. Continue cooking and stirring to 240°F on candy thermometer (soft-ball stage) or until small amount of mixture, when dropped into very cold water, forms a soft ball which flattens when removed from water. (Bulb of candy thermometer should not rest on bottom of saucepan.) Remove from heat. Immediately spoon almond mixture evenly over chips and crust; do not spread.

5 Bake 10 to 15 minutes or just until almond mixture is golden brown. Remove from oven; cool 5 minutes. Sprinkle remaining ½ cup chips over top; cool completely. Cut into bars.

cupcakes & mini cakes

Mini Brownie Cups

MAKES 24 SERVINGS

- ¼ cup (½ stick) light margarine
- 2 egg whites
- 1 egg
- ¾ cup sugar
- ⅔ cup all-purpose flour
- ⅓ cup HERSHEY'S Cocoa
- ½ teaspoon baking powder
- ¼ teaspoon salt
- MOCHA GLAZE (recipe follows)

1 Heat oven to 350°F. Line small muffin cups (1¾ inches in diameter) with paper bake cups or spray with vegetable cooking spray.

2 Melt margarine in small saucepan over low heat; cool slightly. Beat egg whites and egg in small bowl with electric mixer on medium speed until foamy; gradually add sugar, beating until slightly thickened and light in color. Stir together flour, cocoa, baking powder and salt; gradually add to egg mixture, beating until blended. Gradually add melted margarine, beating just until blended. Fill muffin cups ⅔ full with batter.

3 Bake 15 to 18 minutes or until wooden pick inserted in center comes out clean. Remove from pan to wire rack. Cool completely. Prepare MOCHA GLAZE; drizzle over tops of brownie cups. Let stand until glaze is set. Store, covered, at room temperature.

Mocha Glaze

- ¼ cup powdered sugar
- ¾ teaspoon HERSHEY'S Cocoa
- ¼ teaspoon powdered instant coffee
- 2 teaspoons hot water
- ¼ teaspoon vanilla extract

Stir together powdered sugar and cocoa in small bowl. Dissolve instant coffee in water; gradually add to sugar mixture, stirring until well blended. Stir in vanilla.

1ˢᵗ Birthday Cupcakes

- 1⅔ cups all-purpose flour
- 1½ cups sugar
- ½ cup HERSHEY'S Cocoa
- 1½ teaspoons baking soda
- 1 teaspoon salt
- ½ teaspoon baking powder
- 2 eggs
- ½ cup shortening
- 1½ cups buttermilk or sour milk*
- 1 teaspoon vanilla extract
- ONE-BOWL BUTTERCREAM FROSTING (recipe follows)

To sour milk: Use 4½ teaspoons white vinegar plus milk to equal 1½ cups.

1. Heat oven to 350°F. Line muffin cups (2½ inches in diameter) with paper bake cups.

2. Stir together flour, sugar, cocoa, baking soda, salt and baking powder in large bowl. Add eggs, shortening, buttermilk and vanilla. Beat on low speed of mixer 1 minute, scraping bowl constantly. Beat on high speed 3 minutes, scraping bowl occasionally. Fill muffin cups ½ full with batter.

3. Bake 18 to 20 minutes or until wooden pick inserted in center comes out clean. Remove from pan to wire rack. Cool completely. Frost with ONE-BOWL BUTTERCREAM FROSTING.

HERSHEY'S Chocolate Cake: Heat oven to 350°F. Grease two 9-inch round baking pans; line bottoms with wax paper. Prepare batter as directed above; pour into prepared pans. Bake 30 to 35 minutes or until wooden pick inserted in center comes out clean. Cool 10 minutes; remove from pans to wire racks. Remove paper. Cool completely. Frost with ONE-BOWL BUTTERCREAM FROSTING.

One-Bowl Buttercream Frosting

- 6 tablespoons butter or margarine, softened
- 2⅔ cups powdered sugar
- ½ cup HERSHEY'S Cocoa
- ⅓ cup milk
- 1 teaspoon vanilla extract

Beat butter in medium bowl. Add powdered sugar and cocoa alternately with milk and vanilla, beating to spreading consistency (additional milk may be needed).

MAKES ABOUT 2 CUPS FROSTING

Espresso Filled Mini Cakes

MAKES ABOUT 14 MINI CAKES

2   cups sugar

1¾ cups all-purpose flour

¾   cup HERSHEY'S Cocoa

1½ teaspoons baking powder

1½ teaspoons baking soda

1   teaspoon salt

2   eggs

1   cup milk

½   cup vegetable oil

2   teaspoons vanilla extract

1   cup boiling water

ESPRESSO CREAM FILLING (recipe follows) or apricot preserves or other flavor of your choice

COCOA GLAZE (recipe follows)

1 Heat oven to 350°F. Grease and lightly flour fourteen 6-ounce custard cups.

2 Stir together sugar, flour, cocoa, baking powder, baking soda and salt in large bowl. Add eggs, milk, oil and vanilla; beat on medium speed of mixer 2 minutes. Stir in water (batter will be thin). Fill each prepared cup with scant ½ cup batter. Place custard cups on cookie sheet.

3 Bake 20 to 25 minutes or until wooden pick inserted in center comes out clean. Cool 5 minutes on wire racks; remove mini cakes from cups. Cool completely. Cut mini cakes horizontally about 1 inch from top. Spread bottom with ESPRESSO CREAM FILLING or preserves; replace top of cake. Drizzle with COCOA GLAZE. Refrigerate until serving time. Refrigerate leftover cakes.

Espresso Cream Filling: Combine 1 cup (½ pint) cold whipping cream, ¼ cup powdered sugar and 2 teaspoons powdered instant espresso (or powdered instant coffee) in small bowl; beat until stiff. Makes about 2 cups filling.

Cupcakes: Line muffin pan (2½ inches in diameter) with paper bake cups. Fill ½ full with batter. Bake at 350°F. 20 minutes or until wooden pick inserted in center comes out clean. Fill and glaze as directed in recipe. Makes about 3 dozen cupcakes.

Cocoa Glaze

½	**cup whipping cream**
1½	**teaspoons light corn syrup**
½	**cup HERSHEY'S Cocoa**
½	**cup sugar**
1	**tablespoon butter**
1½	**teaspoons vanilla extract**

Stir together whipping cream and corn syrup in small saucepan. Stir together cocoa and sugar in small bowl; add to cream mixture, stirring well. Add butter. Cook over low heat, stirring constantly, until butter melts and mixture is smooth. Do not boil. Remove from heat; stir in vanilla. Cool to desired consistency.

MAKES ABOUT 1 CUP GLAZE

Note: Glaze may be stored in airtight container in refrigerator up to 2 weeks. Reheat over low heat, Stirring constantly.

Glazed Cranberry Mini-Cakes

MAKES ABOUT 3 DOZEN MINI-CAKES

⅓   cup butter or margarine, softened

⅓   cup granulated sugar

⅓   cup packed light brown sugar

1   egg

1¼   teaspoons vanilla extract

1⅓   cups all-purpose flour

¾   teaspoon baking powder

¼   teaspoon baking soda

¼   teaspoon salt

2   tablespoons milk

1¼   cups coarsely chopped fresh cranberries

½   cup coarsely chopped walnuts

1⅔   cups HERSHEY'S Premier White Chips, divided

WHITE GLAZE (recipe follows)

1 Heat oven to 350°F. Lightly grease or paper-line 36 small muffin cups (1¾ inches in diameter).

2 Beat butter, granulated sugar, brown sugar, egg and vanilla in large bowl until fluffy. Stir together flour, baking powder, baking soda and salt; gradually blend into butter mixture. Add milk; stir until blended. Stir in cranberries, walnuts and ⅔ cup white chips (reserve remaining chips for glaze). Fill muffin cups almost full with batter.

3 Bake 18 to 20 minutes or until wooden pick inserted in center comes out clean. Cool 5 minutes; remove from pans to wire rack. Cool completely. Prepare WHITE GLAZE; drizzle over top of mini-cakes. Refrigerate 10 minutes to set glaze.

White Glaze: Place remaining 1 cup HERSHEY'S Premier White Chips in small microwave-safe bowl; sprinkle 2 tablespoons vegetable oil over chips. Microwave at MEDIUM (50%) 30 seconds; stir. If necessary, microwave at MEDIUM an additional 30 seconds or just until chips are melted when stirred.

Molten Chocolate-Cherry Cakes

MAKES 6 SERVINGS

CHOCOLATE DIPPED CHERRIES (recipe follows)

⅔ **cup plus 1 tablespoon sugar, divided**

¾ **cup (1½ sticks) butter or margarine**

½ **cup HERSHEY'S Cocoa**

¼ **cup whipping cream**

1½ **teaspoons vanilla extract**

¼ **cup all-purpose flour**

2 **eggs**

2 **egg yolks**

⅓ **cup maraschino cherries, finely chopped**

Sweetened whipped cream

1 Prepare CHOCOLATE DIPPED CHERRIES.

2 Heat oven to 400°F. Grease six ¾-cup soufflé dishes or six 6-ounce custard cups. Sprinkle insides evenly with 1 tablespoon sugar. Place dishes in 13×9×2-inch baking pan or a jelly-roll pan.

3 Melt butter in medium saucepan. Remove from heat. Whisk in cocoa, ⅓ cup sugar, whipping cream and vanilla. Whisk in flour just until combined. Set aside.

4 Beat eggs, egg yolks and remaining ⅓ cup sugar in large bowl with electric mixer on high speed about 5 minutes or until slightly thickened and lemon-colored. Beat in chocolate mixture on medium speed. Pour about ¼ cup into each prepared custard cup. Sprinkle chopped cherries evenly over each. Carefully pour remaining chocolate mixture into each cup.

5 Bake 13 to 15 minutes or just until top of each cake looks dry. Do not overbake. Let stand in cups 3 minutes. Loosen sides of each. Invert onto serving plates. Serve warm topped with whipped cream and a CHOCOLATE DIPPED CHERRY.

Chocolate Dipped Cherries: Drain 6 maraschino cherries with stems. Pat dry with paper towels. Place ¼ cup HERSHEY'S SPECIAL DARK Chocolate Chips or HERSHEY'S Semi-Sweet Chocolate Chips and ½ teaspoon shortening (do not use butter, margarine, spread or oil) in small microwave-safe bowl. Microwave at MEDIUM (50%) for 45 seconds. Stir until chips are melted. Dip cherries into chocolate mixture. Place on wax paper-lined tray. Refrigerate until serving time.

Tip: For make-ahead convenience, prepare the cakes but do not bake. Cover with plastic wrap and refrigerate for up to 3 hours. Let stand at room temperature 30 minutes, then bake as directed.

P.B. Chips Brownie Cups

MAKES 1½ DOZEN BROWNIE CUPS

1	cup (2 sticks) butter or margarine
2	cups sugar
2	teaspoons vanilla extract
4	eggs
¾	cup HERSHEY'S Cocoa or HERSHEY'S SPECIAL DARK Cocoa
1¾	cups all-purpose flour
½	teaspoon baking powder
½	teaspoon salt
1⅔	cups (10-ounce package) REESE'S Peanut Butter Chips, divided

1 Heat oven to 350°F. Line 18 muffin cups (2½ inches in diameter) with paper or foil bake cups.

2 Place butter in large microwave-safe bowl. Microwave at MEDIUM (50%) 1 to 1½ minutes or until melted. Stir in sugar and vanilla. Add eggs; beat well. Add cocoa; beat until well blended. Add flour, baking powder and salt; beat well. Stir in 1⅓ cups peanut butter chips. Divide batter evenly into muffin cups.

3 Bake 25 to 30 minutes or until surface is firm. Immediately sprinkle remaining ⅓ cup peanut butter chips over muffin tops, pressing in slightly. Cool completely in pan on wire rack.

Filled Rich Chocolate Cupcakes

    FILLING (recipe follows)
3   cups all-purpose flour
2   cups sugar
⅔   cup HERSHEY'S Cocoa
2   teaspoons baking soda
1   teaspoon salt
2   cups water
⅔   cup vegetable oil
2   tablespoons white vinegar
2   teaspoons vanilla extract

1 Prepare FILLING; set aside. Heat oven to 350°F. Line muffin cups (2½ inches in diameter) with paper bake cups.

2 Stir together flour, sugar, cocoa, baking soda and salt in large bowl. Add water, oil, vinegar and vanilla; beat on medium speed of mixer 3 minutes. Fill muffin cups ⅔ full with batter. Spoon 1 level tablespoon FILLING into center of each cupcake.

3 Bake 20 to 25 minutes or until wooden pick inserted in cake portion comes out clean. Remove to wire rack. Cool completely.

Goblin's Delight Filling: Add 2 teaspoons grated orange peel, 4 drops yellow food color and 3 drops red food color to FILLING before stirring in chips.

Valentine Filling: Stir 4 to 5 drops red food color into FILLING.

Peanut Butter Chip Filling: Omit chocolate; stir in 1 cup REESE'S Peanut Butter Chips.

Filling

1   package (8 ounces) cream
    cheese, softened
⅓   cup sugar
1   egg
⅛   teaspoon salt
1   cup HERSHEY'S SPECIAL DARK
    Chocolate Chips, HERSHEY'S
    Semi-Sweet Chocolate Chips or
    HERSHEY'S Mini Chips Semi-
    Sweet Chocolate

Beat cream cheese, sugar, egg and salt in small bowl; beat until smooth and creamy. Stir in chocolate chips.

Mini Cocoa Cupcake Kabobs

MAKES ABOUT 4 DOZEN CUPCAKES

1	**cup sugar**
1	**cup all-purpose flour**
⅓	**cup HERSHEY'S Cocoa**
¾	**teaspoon baking powder**
¾	**teaspoon baking soda**
½	**teaspoon salt**
1	**egg**
½	**cup milk**
¼	**cup vegetable oil**
1	**teaspoon vanilla extract**
½	**cup boiling water**

LICKETY-SPLIT COCOA FROSTING (recipe follows)

Jelly beans or sugar nonpareils and/or decorating frosting

Marshmallows

Strawberries

Wooden or metal skewers

1 Heat oven to 350°F. Spray small muffin cups (1¾ inches in diameter) with vegetable cooking spray.

2 Stir together sugar, flour, cocoa, baking powder, baking soda and salt in medium bowl. Add egg, milk, oil and vanilla; beat on medium speed of mixer 2 minutes. Stir in boiling water (batter will be thin). Fill muffin cups about ⅔ full with batter.

3 Bake 10 minutes or until wooden pick inserted in center comes out clean. Cool slightly; remove from pans to wire racks. Cool completely. Frost with LICKETY-SPLIT COCOA FROSTING. Garnish with jelly beans, nonpareils and/or frosting piped onto cupcake. Alternate cupcakes, marshmallows and strawberries on skewers.

Lickety-Split Cocoa Frosting:
Beat 3 tablespoons softened butter or margarine in small bowl until creamy. Add 1¼ cups powdered sugar, ¼ cup HERSHEY'S Cocoa, 2 to 3 tablespoons milk and ½ teaspoon vanilla extract until smooth and of desired consistency. Makes about 1 cup frosting.

Note: Number of kabobs will be determined by length of skewer used and number of cupcakes, marshmallows and strawberries placed on each skewer.

Toffee Topped Pineapple Upside-Down Cakes

¼ cup light corn syrup

¼ cup (½ stick) butter or margarine, melted

1 cup HEATH BITS 'O BRICKLE Toffee Bits

4 pineapple rings

4 maraschino cherries

¼ cup (½ stick) butter or margarine, softened

⅔ cup sugar

1 egg

1 tablespoon rum or 1 teaspoon rum extract

1⅓ cups all-purpose flour

2 teaspoons baking powder

⅔ cup milk

1 Heat oven to 350°F. Lightly coat inside of 4 individual 2-cup baking dishes with vegetable oil spray.

2 Stir together 1 tablespoon corn syrup and 1 tablespoon melted butter in each of 4 baking dishes. Sprinkle each with ¼ cup toffee. Center pineapple rings on toffee and place cherries in centers.

3 Beat softened butter and sugar in small bowl until blended. Add egg and rum, beating well. Stir together flour and baking powder; add alternately with milk to butter-sugar mixture, beating until smooth. Spoon about ¾ cup batter into each prepared dish.

4 Bake 25 to 30 minutes or until wooden pick inserted in centers comes out clean. Immediately invert onto serving dishes; cool slightly before serving. Refrigerate leftovers.

party time treats

Midnight Chocolate Cheesecake Cookie Cups

MAKES 30 DESSERT CUPS

- ¼ **cup (½ stick) butter, softened**
- ¼ **cup shortening**
- ½ **cup sugar**
- 1 **egg**
- ½ **teaspoon vanilla extract**
- 1 **cup all-purpose flour**
- 2 **tablespoons HERSHEY'S SPECIAL DARK Cocoa or HERSHEY'S Cocoa**
- ½ **teaspoon baking powder**
- ⅛ **teaspoon salt**
- **CHOCOLATE FILLING (recipe follows)**
- **Whipped topping or sweetened whipped cream**
- 30 **HERSHEY'S KISSES**BRAND **SPECIAL DARK Mildly Sweet Chocolates, unwrapped**

1 Heat oven to 350°F. Paper or foil line 30 small (1 ¾-inch diameter) muffin cups.

2 Beat butter and shortening in medium bowl until fluffy. Beat in sugar, egg and vanilla. Stir together flour, cocoa, baking powder and salt. Gradually blend into butter mixture, blending well.

3 Drop rounded teaspoonful of dough into each prepared muffin cup. Using back of spoon, push dough up sides of muffin cup forming crater in cup. (If you have difficulty with this step, refrigerate pans for about 10 minutes and then continue.) Prepare CHOCOLATE FILLING; evenly divide into muffin cups. (Cups will be very full.)

4 Bake 15 minutes or until cheesecake is set. Cool completely in pan on wire rack. Cover; refrigerate until ready to serve. To serve, top each cheesecake with whipped topping rosette and chocolate piece.

Chocolate Filling: Beat 2 packages (3 ounces each) softened cream cheese and ¼ cup sugar until well blended. Beat in 1 egg, 1 teaspoon vanilla extract and ⅛ teaspoon salt. Place 12 unwrapped HERSHEY'S KISSESBRAND SPECIAL DARK Mildly Sweet Chocolates in small microwave-safe bowl. Microwave at MEDIUM (50%) 15 seconds at a time, stirring after each heating, until chocolates are melted and smooth when stirred. Cool slightly, blend into cheesecake batter.

Peanut Butter Cup Rocky Road Squares

MAKES ABOUT 20 SERVINGS

38	to 40 REESE'S Peanut Butter Cups Miniatures
1	cup (2 sticks) butter or margarine
1¼	cups HERSHEY'S Cocoa, divided
2	cups sugar
4	eggs
2½	teaspoons vanilla extract, divided
1¾	cups all-purpose flour
1	can (14 ounces) sweetened condensed milk (not evaporated milk)
1	jar (7 ounces) marshmallow crème
½	cup coarsely chopped peanuts

1 Heat oven to 350°F. Line 13×9×2-inch baking pan with foil, extending foil beyond sides. Grease foil. Remove wrappers from peanut butter cups. Cut each peanut butter cup into 4 pieces; set aside.

2 Place butter in large microwave-safe bowl. Microwave at MEDIUM (50%) 1 minute or until butter is melted. Stir in ¾ cup cocoa until smooth. Add sugar, 3 eggs and 1 teaspoon vanilla; blend well. Blend in flour; spread in prepared pan. Bake 15 minutes.

3 Meanwhile, combine sweetened condensed milk, remaining ½ cup cocoa, remaining egg and remaining 1½ teaspoons vanilla. Pour over baked layer. Return to oven; bake 20 to 25 minutes or until set.

4 Place marshmallow crème by heaping teaspoonfuls over hot surface. Allow to soften about 5 minutes; carefully spread over surface. Immediately sprinkle peanut butter cup pieces and peanuts over marshmallow. Cool completely in pan on wire rack. Refrigerate until thoroughly chilled.

5 Lift dessert from pan using foil as handles; place on cutting board. Cut into squares. To serve, gently heat in microwave at MEDIUM about 10 seconds or 200°F oven until marshmallow softens. (Dessert may also be allowed to soften at room temperature until ready to serve.) Cover; refrigerate leftovers.

Holiday Red Raspberry Chocolate Bars

MAKES 36 BARS

- 2½ cups all-purpose flour
- 1 cup sugar
- ¾ cup finely chopped pecans
- 1 egg, beaten
- 1 cup (2 sticks) cold butter or margarine
- 1 jar (12 ounces) seedless red raspberry jam
- 1⅔ cups HERSHEY'S Milk Chocolate Chips, HERSHEY'S SPECIAL DARK Chocolate Chips, HERSHEY'S Semi-Sweet Chocolate Chips or HERSHEY'S MINI KISSES BRAND Milk Chocolates

1 Heat oven to 350°F. Grease 13×9×2-inch baking pan.

2 Stir together flour, sugar, pecans and egg in large bowl. Cut in butter with pastry blender or fork until mixture resembles coarse crumbs; set aside 1½ cups crumb mixture. Press remaining crumb mixture on bottom of prepared pan. Stir jam to soften; carefully spread over crumb mixture in pan. Sprinkle with chocolate chips. Crumble reserved crumb mixture evenly over top.

3 Bake 40 to 45 minutes or until lightly browned. Cool completely in pan on wire rack; cut into bars.

Brownie Petit Fours

MAKES ABOUT 3 DOZEN PETIT FOURS

½ cup (1 stick) butter or margarine, melted

1 cup sugar

1 teaspoon vanilla extract

2 eggs

½ cup all-purpose flour

⅓ cup HERSHEY'S Cocoa

¼ teaspoon baking powder

¼ teaspoon salt

½ cup chopped walnuts (optional)

2 cups (12-ounce package) HERSHEY'S Mini Chips Semi-Sweet Chocolate

3 tablespoons shortening (do not use butter, margarine, spread or oil)

Sprinkles or decorator's icing (optional)

1 Heat oven to 350°F. Line 9-inch square baking pan with foil; grease foil.

2 Stir together butter, sugar and vanilla in bowl. Add eggs; beat well with spoon. Stir together flour, cocoa, baking powder and salt; gradually add to egg mixture, beating until well blended. Stir in walnuts, if desired. Spread batter evenly in prepared pan.

3 Bake 20 to 25 minutes or until brownie begins to pull away from sides of pan. Cool completely in pan on wire rack; refrigerate about 2 hours.

4 Using edges of foil, lift brownie out of pan. Peel off foil; cut into 1¼-inch squares and allow to warm up to room temperature.

5 Line tray with wax paper. Melt small chocolate chips and shortening in small heavy saucepan over very low heat. Dip each brownie square into melted chocolate, covering completely. (Return to heat if chocolate cools and is hard to coat.) Gently tap on side of pan to allow extra chocolate to drip off. Place on prepared tray. Allow chocolate to set at room temperature or refrigerate until set (about 30 minutes); decorate as desired. (Sprinkles should be added just before chocolate sets.)

Creamy Filled Brownies

½ cup (1 stick) butter or margarine

⅓ cup HERSHEY'S Cocoa

2 eggs

1 cup sugar

½ cup all-purpose flour

¼ teaspoon baking powder

¼ teaspoon salt

1 teaspoon vanilla extract

1 cup finely chopped nuts

CREAMY FILLING (recipe follows)

MINI CHIP GLAZE (recipe follows)

½ cup sliced almonds or chopped nuts (optional)

1 Heat oven to 350°F. Line 15½ × 10½ × 1-inch jelly-roll pan with foil; grease foil.

2 Melt butter in small saucepan; remove from heat. Stir in cocoa until smooth. Beat eggs in medium bowl; gradually add sugar, beating until fluffy. Stir together flour, baking powder and salt; add to egg mixture. Add cocoa mixture and vanilla; beat well. Stir in 1 cup chopped nuts. Spread batter in prepared pan.

3 Bake 12 to 14 minutes or until top springs back when touched lightly in center. Cool completely in pan on wire rack; remove from pan to cutting board. Remove foil; cut brownie in half crosswise. Spread one half with CREAMY FILLING; top with second half. Spread MINI CHIP GLAZE over top; sprinkle with sliced almonds, if desired. After glaze has set, cut into bars.

Creamy Filling: Beat 1 package (3 ounces) softened cream cheese, 2 tablespoons softened butter or margarine and 1 teaspoon vanilla extract in small bowl. Gradually add 1 ½ cups powdered sugar, beating until of spreading consistency.

Filling Variations: Coffee: Add 1 teaspoon powdered instant coffee. **Orange:** Add ½ teaspoon freshly grated orange peel and 1 or 2 drops orange food color. **Almond:** Add ¼ teaspoon almond extract.

Mini Chip Glaze: Heat ¼ cup sugar and 2 tablespoons water to boiling in small saucepan. Remove from heat. Immediately add ½ cup HERSHEY'S Mini Chips Semi-Sweet Chocolate, stirring until melted.

Marbled Cherry Brownies

MAKES ABOUT 16 BROWNIES

CHERRY CREAM FILLING (recipe follows)

½ **cup (1 stick) butter or margarine, melted**

⅓ **cup HERSHEY'S Cocoa**

2 **eggs**

1 **cup sugar**

1 **teaspoon vanilla extract**

½ **cup all-purpose flour**

½ **teaspoon baking powder**

¼ **teaspoon salt**

1 Prepare CHERRY CREAM FILLING; set aside. Heat oven to 350°F. Grease 9-inch square baking pan.

2 Stir butter and cocoa in small bowl until well blended. Beat eggs in medium bowl until foamy. Gradually add sugar and vanilla, beating until well blended. Stir together flour, baking powder and salt; add to egg mixture. Add cocoa mixture; stir until well blended.

3 Spread half of chocolate batter in prepared pan; cover with CHERRY CREAM FILLING. Drop spoonfuls of remaining chocolate batter over filling. With knife or spatula, gently swirl chocolate batter into filling for marbled effect.

4 Bake 35 to 40 minutes or until brownies begin to pull away from sides of pan. Cool; cut into squares. Cover; refrigerate leftover brownies. Bring to room temperature to serve.

Cherry Cream Filling

1 **package (3 ounces) cream cheese, softened**

¼ **cup sugar**

1 **egg**

½ **teaspoon vanilla extract**

¼ **teaspoon almond extract**

⅓ **cup chopped maraschino cherries, well drained**

1 **to 2 drops red food color (optional)**

1 Beat cream cheese and sugar in small bowl on medium speed of mixer until blended. Add egg, vanilla and almond extract; beat well. (Mixture will be thin.)

2 Stir in cherries and food color, if desired.

Patriotic Cocoa Cupcakes

2   **cups sugar**

1¾   **cups all-purpose flour**

¾   **cup HERSHEY'S Cocoa**

2   **teaspoons baking soda**

1   **teaspoon baking powder**

1   **teaspoon salt**

2   **eggs**

1   **cup buttermilk or sour milk***

1   **cup boiling water**

½   **cup vegetable oil**

1   **teaspoon vanilla extract**

    VANILLA FROSTING (recipe follows)

    Chocolate stars or blue and red decorating icings (in tubes)

To sour milk: Use 1 tablespoon white vinegar plus milk to equal 1 cup.

1 Heat oven to 350°F. Grease and flour muffin cups (2½ inches in diameter) or line with paper bake cups.

2 Combine dry ingredients in large bowl. Add eggs, buttermilk, water, oil and vanilla; beat on medium speed of mixer 2 minutes (batter will be thin). Fill cups ⅔ full with batter.

3 Bake 15 minutes or until wooden pick inserted in center comes out clean. Remove cupcakes from pan. Cool completely. To make chocolate stars for garnish, if desired, cut several cupcakes into ½-inch slices; cut out star shapes from cake slices. Frost remaining cupcakes. Garnish with chocolate stars or with blue and red decorating icings.

Vanilla Frosting: Beat ¼ cup (½ stick) softened butter, ¼ cup shortening and 2 teaspoons vanilla extract in large bowl. Add 1 cup powdered sugar; beat until creamy. Add 3 cups powdered sugar alternately with 3 to 4 tablespoons milk, beating to spreading consistency. Makes about 2⅓ cups frosting.

Witch's Hat Chocolate Cupcakes

MAKES ABOUT 2½ DOZEN CUPCAKES

¾ cup (1½ sticks) butter or margarine, softened

1⅔ cups sugar

3 eggs

1 teaspoon vanilla extract

2 cups all-purpose flour

⅔ cup HERSHEY'S Cocoa

1¼ teaspoons baking soda

1 teaspoon salt

¼ teaspoon baking powder

1⅓ cups water

ORANGE CREAM FILLING (recipe follows)

1 Heat oven to 350°F. Line muffin cups (2½ inches in diameter) with paper bake cups.

2 Combine butter, sugar, eggs and vanilla in large bowl; beat on medium speed of mixer 3 minutes. Stir together flour, cocoa, baking soda, salt and baking powder; add alternately with water to butter mixture, beating after each addition until just blended. Fill muffin cups ⅔ full with batter.

3 Bake 20 to 25 minutes or until wooden pick inserted in center comes out clean. Remove from pans to wire racks. Cool completely.

4 Prepare ORANGE CREAM FILLING. Cut 1½-inch cone-shaped piece from center of each cupcake; reserve. Fill each cavity with scant tablespoon prepared filling. Place reserved cake pieces on filling, pointed side up. Refrigerate before serving. Cover; refrigerate leftover filled cupcakes.

Orange Cream Filling

½ cup (1 stick) butter or margarine, softened

1 cup marshmallow crème

1¼ cups powdered sugar

½ to 1 teaspoon freshly grated orange peel

½ teaspoon vanilla extract

2 to 3 teaspoons orange juice

Red and yellow food colors (optional)

Beat butter in small bowl until creamy; gradually beat in marshmallow crème. Gradually add powdered sugar, orange peel and vanilla, beating until blended. Add orange juice and food colors, if desired; beat until smooth and of desired consistency.

MAKES ABOUT 1⅓ CUPS FILLING

Sweetheart Layer Bars

MAKES ABOUT 36 BARS

1	cup (2 sticks) butter or margarine, divided
1½	cups finely crushed unsalted thin pretzels or pretzel sticks
1	cup HERSHEY'S MINI KISSES BRAND Milk Chocolates
1	can (14 ounces) sweetened condensed milk (not evaporated milk)
¾	cup HERSHEY'S Cocoa
2	cups MOUNDS Sweetened Coconut Flakes, tinted*

To tint coconut: Place 1 teaspoon water and ½ teaspoon red food color in small bowl; stir in 2 cups coconut flakes. With fork, toss until evenly coated.

1 Heat oven to 350°F.

2 Place ¾ cup butter (1½ sticks) in 13×9×2-inch baking pan; place in oven just until butter melts. Remove from oven. Stir in crushed pretzels; press evenly onto bottom of pan. Sprinkle chocolates over pretzel layer.

3 Place sweetened condensed milk, cocoa and remaining ¼ cup butter (½ stick) in small microwave-safe bowl. Microwave at MEDIUM (50%) 1 to 1½ minutes or until mixture is melted and smooth when stirred; carefully pour over chocolate layer in pan. Top with coconut; press firmly down onto chocolate layer.

4 Bake 25 to 30 minutes or until lightly browned around edges. Cool completely in pan on wire rack. Cut into heart-shaped pieces with cookie cutters or cut into bars.

Easter Baskets and Bunnies Cupcakes

MAKES ABOUT 33 CUPCAKES

2	cups sugar
1¾	cups all-purpose flour
¾	cup HERSHEY'S Cocoa or HERSHEY'S SPECIAL DARK Cocoa
1½	teaspoons baking powder
1½	teaspoons baking soda
1	teaspoon salt
2	eggs
1	cup milk
½	cup vegetable oil
2	teaspoons vanilla extract
1	cup boiling water
	CREAMY VANILLA FROSTING (recipe follows)*
	Green, red and yellow food color
3¾	cups MOUNDS Sweetened Coconut Flakes, divided and tinted**
	Suggested garnishes: marshmallows, HERSHEY'S MINI KISSES_{BRAND} Milk Chocolates, licorice, jelly beans

Substitute 1 can (16 ounces) creamy vanilla ready-to-spread frosting, if desired.

**To tint coconut: Combine ¾ teaspoon water with several drops green food color in small bowl; stir in 1¼ cups coconut flakes. With fork, toss until evenly tinted. Repeat with red and yellow food color and remaining coconut.*

1 Heat oven to 350°F. Line muffin cups (2½ inches in diameter) with paper bake cups.

2 Stir together sugar, flour, cocoa, baking powder, baking soda and salt in large bowl. Add eggs, milk, oil and vanilla; beat on medium speed of mixer 2 minutes. Stir in boiling water (batter will be thin). Fill muffin cups ⅔ full with batter.

3 Bake 22 to 25 minutes or until wooden pick inserted in center comes out clean. Cool completely. Prepare CREAMY VANILLA FROSTING; frost cupcakes. Immediately press desired color tinted coconut onto each cupcake. Garnish as desired to resemble Easter basket or bunny.

Creamy Vanilla Frosting: Beat ⅓ cup softened butter or margarine in medium bowl. Add 1 cup powdered sugar and 1½ teaspoons vanilla extract; beat well. Add 2½ cups powdered sugar alternately with ¼ cup milk, beating to spreading consistency. Makes about 2 cups frosting.

Touchdown Brownie Cups

MAKES ABOUT 17 CUPCAKES

1	**cup (2 sticks) butter or margarine**
½	**cup HERSHEY'S Cocoa or HERSHEY'S SPECIAL DARK Cocoa**
1	**cup packed light brown sugar**
½	**cup granulated sugar**
3	**eggs**
1	**teaspoon vanilla extract**
1	**cup all-purpose flour**
1⅓	**cups chopped pecans, divided**

1 Heat oven to 350°F. Line 2½-inch muffin cups with foil or paper bake cups.

2 Place butter in large microwave-safe bowl; cover. Microwave at MEDIUM (50%) 1½ minutes or until melted. Add cocoa; stir until smooth. Add brown sugar and granulated sugar; stir until well blended. Add eggs and vanilla; beat well. Add flour and 1 cup pecans; stir until well blended. Fill prepared muffin cups about ¾ full of batter; sprinkle about 1 teaspoon remaining pecans over top of each.

3 Bake 20 to 25 minutes or until tops begin to dry and crack. Cool completely in cups on wire rack.

contents

COOKIES, CANDIES & SNACKS

94

114

124

140

all-time favorites

Peanut Butter Blossoms

MAKES ABOUT 4 DOZEN COOKIES

48	HERSHEY'S KISSES_{BRAND} Milk Chocolates
¾	cup REESE'S Creamy Peanut Butter
½	cup shortening
⅓	cup granulated sugar
⅓	cup packed light brown sugar
1	egg
2	tablespoons milk
1	teaspoon vanilla extract
1½	cups all-purpose flour
1	teaspoon baking soda
½	teaspoon salt
	Granulated sugar

1 Heat oven to 375°F. Remove wrappers from chocolates.

2 Beat peanut butter and shortening with electric mixer on medium speed in large bowl until well blended. Add ⅓ cup granulated sugar and brown sugar; beat until fluffy. Add egg, milk and vanilla; beat well. Stir together flour, baking soda and salt; gradually beat into peanut butter mixture.

3 Shape dough into 1-inch balls. Roll in additional granulated sugar; place on ungreased cookie sheet.

4 Bake 8 to 10 minutes or until lightly browned. Immediately press a chocolate into center of each cookie; cookies will crack around edges. Remove to wire racks and cool completely.

Fudgey German Chocolate Sandwich Cookies

MAKES ABOUT 17 SANDWICH COOKIES

1¾ cups all-purpose flour

1½ cups sugar

¾ cup (1½ sticks) butter or margarine, softened

⅔ cup HERSHEY'S Cocoa or HERSHEY'S SPECIAL DARK Cocoa

¾ teaspoon baking soda

¼ teaspoon salt

2 eggs

2 tablespoons milk

1 teaspoon vanilla extract

½ cup finely chopped pecans

COCONUT AND PECAN FILLING (recipe follows)

1 Heat oven to 350°F.

2 Combine flour, sugar, butter, cocoa, baking soda, salt, eggs, milk and vanilla in large bowl. Beat at medium speed of mixer until blended (batter will be stiff). Stir in pecans.

3 Form dough into 1¼-inch balls. Place on ungreased cookie sheet; flatten slightly.

4 Bake 9 to 11 minutes or until almost set. Cool slightly; remove from cookie sheet to wire rack. Cool completely. Spread about 1 heaping tablespoon COCONUT AND PECAN FILLING onto bottom of one cookie. Top with second cookie to make sandwich. Serve warm or at room temperature.

Note: Cookies can be reheated in microwave. Microwave at HIGH (100%) 10 seconds or until filling is warm.

Coconut and Pecan Filling

½ cup (1 stick) butter or margarine

½ cup packed light brown sugar

¼ cup light corn syrup

1 cup MOUNDS Sweetened Coconut Flakes, toasted*

1 cup finely chopped pecans

1 teaspoon vanilla extract

To toast coconut: Heat oven to 350°F. Spread coconut in even layer on baking sheet. Bake 6 to 8 minutes, stirring occasionally, until golden.

Melt butter in medium saucepan over medium heat; add brown sugar and corn syrup. Stir constantly until thick and bubbly. Remove from heat; stir in coconut, pecans and vanilla. Use warm.

MAKES ABOUT 2 CUPS FILLING

Chocolate Chip & Toffee Bits Cookies

MAKES ABOUT 4 DOZEN COOKIES

- 2¼ cups all-purpose flour
- 1 teaspoon baking soda
- ½ teaspoon salt
- ¾ cup (1½ sticks) butter or margarine, softened
- ¾ cup granulated sugar
- ¾ cup packed light brown sugar
- 1 teaspoon vanilla extract
- 2 eggs
- 1 cup HEATH BITS 'O BRICKLE Toffee Bits
- 1 cup HERSHEY'S SPECIAL DARK Chocolate Chips or HERSHEY'S Semi-Sweet Chocolate Chips

1 Heat oven to 375°F.

2 Stir together flour, baking soda and salt in medium bowl. Beat butter, granulated sugar, brown sugar and vanilla in large bowl until well blended. Add eggs; beat well. Gradually add flour mixture, beating well. Stir in toffee bits and chocolate chips. Drop dough by rounded teaspoons onto ungreased cookie sheet.

3 Bake 8 to 10 minutes or until lightly browned. Cool slightly; remove from cookie sheet to wire rack. Cool completely.

HERSHEY'S Double Chocolate MINI KISSES Cookies

MAKES ABOUT 3½ DOZEN COOKIES

1	cup (2 sticks) butter or margarine, softened
1½	cups sugar
2	eggs
2	teaspoons vanilla extract
2	cups all-purpose flour
⅔	cup HERSHEY'S Cocoa
¾	teaspoon baking soda
¼	teaspoon salt
1¾	cups (10-ounce package) HERSHEY'S MINI KISSESBRAND Milk Chocolates
½	cup coarsely chopped nuts (optional)

1 Heat oven to 350°F.

2 Beat butter, sugar, eggs and vanilla with electric mixer on medium speed in large bowl until light and fluffy. Stir together flour, cocoa, baking soda and salt; add to butter mixture, beating until well blended. Stir in chocolates and nuts, if desired. Drop by tablespoons onto ungreased cookie sheet.

3 Bake 8 to 10 minutes or just until set. Cool slightly. Remove to wire rack and cool completely.

HERSHEY'S SPECIAL DARK Chip and Macadamia Nut Cookies

MAKES 3½ DOZEN COOKIES

6	tablespoons butter, softened
⅓	cup butter-flavored shortening
½	cup packed light brown sugar
⅓	cup granulated sugar
1	egg
1½	teaspoons vanilla extract
1⅓	cups all-purpose flour
½	teaspoon baking soda
½	teaspoon salt
2	cups (12-ounce package) HERSHEY'S SPECIAL DARK Chocolate Chips
½	cup MAUNA LOA Macadamia Nut Baking Pieces

1 Heat oven to 350°F.

2 Beat butter and shortening in large bowl until well blended. Add brown sugar and granulated sugar; beat thoroughly. Add egg and vanilla, beating until well blended. Stir together flour, baking soda and salt; gradually beat into butter mixture. Stir in chocolate chips and nuts. Drop by rounded teaspoons onto ungreased cookie sheet.

3 Bake 10 to 12 minutes or until edges are lightly browned. Cool slightly; transfer to wire rack. Cool completely.

White Chips and Macadamia Pieces Cookies: Substitute 2 cups (12-ounce package) HERSHEY'S Premier White Chips for HERSHEY'S SPECIAL DARK Chocolate Chips. Prepare as directed above.

Chocolate Cookies: Decrease flour to 1 cup; add ⅓ cup HERSHEY'S Cocoa or HERSHEY'S SPECIAL DARK Cocoa.

Oatmeal Toffee Cookies

MAKES ABOUT 4 DOZEN COOKIES

1	cup (2 sticks) butter or margarine, softened
2	cups packed light brown sugar
2	eggs
2	teaspoons vanilla extract
1¾	cups all-purpose flour
1	teaspoon baking soda
1	teaspoon ground cinnamon
½	teaspoon salt
3	cups quick-cooking oats
1⅓	cups (8-ounce package) HEATH BITS 'O BRICKLE Toffee Bits
1	cup MOUNDS Sweetened Coconut Flakes (optional)

1 Heat oven to 375°F. Lightly grease cookie sheet or line with parchment paper.

2 Beat butter, brown sugar, eggs and vanilla with electric mixer on medium speed in large bowl until well blended. Add flour, baking soda, cinnamon and salt; beat until blended. Stir in oats, toffee bits and coconut, if desired, with spoon. Drop dough by rounded teaspoons about 2 inches apart onto prepared sheet.

3 Bake 8 to 10 minutes or until edges are lightly browned. Cool 1 minute. Remove to wire rack and cool completely.

Design Your Own Chocolate Cookie

MAKES ABOUT 5 DOZEN COOKIES

- **1** cup (2 sticks) butter, softened
- **1** cup granulated sugar
- **¾** cup packed light brown sugar
- **2** teaspoons vanilla extract
- **½** teaspoon salt
- **2** eggs
- **2** cups all-purpose flour
- **½** cup HERSHEY'S Cocoa
- **1** teaspoon baking soda

1 Heat oven to 375°F.

2 Beat butter, granulated sugar, brown sugar, vanilla and salt in large bowl until creamy. Add eggs; beat well.

3 Stir together flour, cocoa and baking soda; gradually add to butter mixture, beating until well blended. Drop by rounded teaspoons onto ungreased cookie sheet.

4 Bake 8 to 10 minutes or until set. Cool slightly; remove from cookie sheet to wire rack. Cool completely.

Chocolate Chocolate Chip Cookies: Add 2 cups (12-ounce package) HERSHEY'S SPECIAL DARK Chocolate Chips, Semi-Sweet Chocolate Chips or Mini Chips Semi-Sweet Chocolate or 2 cups (11.5-ounce package) HERSHEY'S Milk Chocolate Chips to basic chocolate batter.

MINI KISSES Chocolate Cookies: Add 1¾ cups (10-ounce package) HERSHEY'S MINI KISSESBRAND Milk Chocolates to basic chocolate batter.

Mint Chocolate Chip Cookies: Add 1⅔ cups (10-ounce package) HERSHEY'S Mint Chocolate Chips to basic chocolate batter.

Chocolate Cookies with White Chips: Add 2 cups (12-ounce package) HERSHEY'S Premier White Chips to basic chocolate batter.

Chocolate Cookies with Peanut Butter Chips: Add 1⅔ cups (10-ounce package) REESE'S Peanut Butter Chips to basic chocolate batter.

Chocolate Cookies with Toffee: Add 1 to 1¼ cups HEATH BITS 'O BRICKLE Toffee Bits or HEATH Milk Chocolate Toffee Bits to basic chocolate batter. Lightly grease or paper-line cookie sheets.

Oatmeal Butterscotch Cookies

MAKES ABOUT 4 DOZEN COOKIES

¾ cup (1½ sticks) butter or margarine, softened

¾ cup granulated sugar

¾ cup packed light brown sugar

2 eggs

1 teaspoon vanilla extract

1¼ cups all-purpose flour

1 teaspoon baking soda

½ teaspoon salt

½ teaspoon ground cinnamon

3 cups quick-cooking or regular rolled oats, uncooked

1¾ cups (11-ounce package) HERSHEY'S Butterscotch Chips

1 Heat oven to 375°F.

2 Beat butter, granulated sugar and brown sugar in large bowl with electric mixer on medium speed until well blended. Add eggs and vanilla; blend thoroughly. Stir together flour, baking soda, salt and cinnamon; gradually add to butter mixture, beating until well blended. Stir in oats and butterscotch chips; mix well. Drop by heaping teaspoons onto ungreased cookie sheet.

3 Bake 8 to 10 minutes or until golden brown. Cool slightly on pan. Remove to wire rack and cool completely.

HERSHEY'S MINI KISSES
Milk Chocolate Peanut Butter Cookies

MAKES 1½ DOZEN COOKIES

- ¼ cup (½ stick) butter or margarine, softened
- ¼ cup REESE'S Creamy Peanut Butter
- ¼ cup granulated sugar
- ¼ cup packed light brown sugar
- 1 egg
- ½ teaspoon vanilla extract
- ⅔ cup all-purpose flour
- ¼ teaspoon baking soda
- ⅛ teaspoon salt
- 1¾ cups (10-ounce package) HERSHEY'S MINI KISSESBRAND Milk Chocolates

1 Heat oven to 350°F. Lightly grease cookie sheet or line with parchment paper.

2 Beat butter and peanut butter in large bowl on medium speed of electric mixer until creamy. Gradually add granulated sugar and brown sugar, beating until well mixed. Add egg and vanilla; beat until light and fluffy. Stir together flour, baking soda and salt; add to butter mixture, beating until well blended. Stir in chocolates. Drop batter by rounded tablespoons onto prepared cookie sheet.

3 Bake 10 to 12 minutes or until lightly browned. Cool slightly; remove from cookie sheet to wire rack. Cool completely.

refrigerated & cut-out cookies

Rich Cocoa Crinkle Cookies

MAKES ABOUT 6 DOZEN COOKIES

- 2 cups granulated sugar
- ¾ cup vegetable oil
- 1 cup HERSHEY'S Cocoa
- 4 eggs
- 2 teaspoons vanilla extract
- 2⅓ cups all-purpose flour
- 2 teaspoons baking powder
- ½ teaspoon salt
- Powdered sugar

1 Combine granulated sugar and oil in large bowl; add cocoa, beating until well blended. Beat in eggs and vanilla. Stir together flour, baking powder and salt. Gradually add to cocoa mixture, beating well.

2 Cover; refrigerate until dough is firm enough to handle, at least 6 hours.

3 Heat oven to 350°F. Lightly grease cookie sheet or line with parchment paper. Shape dough into 1-inch balls; roll in powdered sugar to coat. Place about 2 inches apart on prepared cookie sheet.

4 Bake 10 to 12 minutes or until almost no indentation remains when touched lightly and tops are crackled. Cool slightly. Remove from cookie sheet to wire rack. Cool completely.

Almond Shortbread Cookies with Chocolate Filling

MAKES ABOUT 44 SANDWICH COOKIES

¾ cup sliced almonds, toasted*

1 cup (2 sticks) butter or margarine, softened

¾ cup granulated sugar

3 egg yolks

¾ teaspoon almond extract

2 cups all-purpose flour

CHOCOLATE FILLING (recipe follows)

Powdered sugar (optional)

To toast almonds: Heat oven to 350°F. Spread almonds in thin layer in shallow baking pan. Bake 8 to 10 minutes, stirring occasionally, until light golden brown; cool.

1 Finely chop almonds; set aside.

2 Beat butter and granulated sugar in large bowl until creamy. Add egg yolks and almond extract; beat well. Gradually add flour, beating until well blended. Stir in almonds. Refrigerate dough 1 to 2 hours or until firm enough to handle.

3 Heat oven to 350°F. On well-floured surface, roll about ¼ of dough to about ⅛-inch thickness (keep remaining dough in refrigerator). Using 2-inch round cookie cutter, cut into equal number of rounds. Place on ungreased cookie sheet. Repeat with remaining dough.

4 Bake 8 to 10 minutes or until almost set. Cool slightly; remove from cookie sheet to wire rack. Cool completely. Spread about 1 measuring teaspoonful CHOCOLATE FILLING onto bottom of one cookie. Top with second cookie; gently press together. Repeat with remaining cookies. Allow to set, about 1 hour. Lightly sift powdered sugar over top of cookies, if desired. Cover; store at room temperature.

Chocolate Filling: Combine 1 cup HERSHEY'S Milk Chocolate Chips** and ⅓ cup whipping cream in small saucepan. Stir constantly over low heat until mixture is smooth. Remove from heat. Cool about 20 minutes or until slightly thickened and spreadable. Makes about 1 cup filling.

**HERSHEY'S SPECIAL DARK Chocolate Chips or HERSHEY'S Semi-Sweet Chocolate Chips may also be used.*

Double Chocolate Peanut Butter Sandwich Cookies

MAKES ABOUT 25 SANDWICH COOKIES

1¾ cups all-purpose flour

1½ cups sugar

¾ cup (1½ sticks) butter or margarine, softened

⅔ cup HERSHEY'S Cocoa

¾ teaspoon baking soda

2 eggs

2 tablespoons milk

1 teaspoon vanilla extract

CHOCOLATE FOR DIPPING (recipe follows)

¼ cup finely chopped peanuts (optional)

1¾ cups REESE'S Creamy Peanut Butter

1 Heat oven to 350°F.

2 Combine flour, sugar, butter, cocoa, baking soda, eggs, milk and vanilla in large mixing bowl; beat until well blended. Refrigerate until firm enough to handle, about 2 hours. Roll chilled batter into 1-inch balls; place on ungreased cookie sheet.

3 Bake 8 to 10 minutes or until almost set. Cool slightly; remove from cookie sheet to wire rack. Cool completely.

4 Line tray or cookie sheet with wax paper. Prepare CHOCOLATE FOR DIPPING. Dip half of cookies into prepared coating, covering one-half of each cookie. Place on prepared tray. Sprinkle peanuts over top of cookies, if desired; let stand until chocolate is set.

5 Spread about 1 tablespoon peanut butter on flat side of remaining cookies; top with dipped cookies, pressing down gently. Tightly cover; store at room temperature.

Chocolate for Dipping: Place 1 cup HERSHEY'S SPECIAL DARK Chocolate Chips or HERSHEY'S Semi-Sweet Chocolate Chips and 1 teaspoon shortening (do not use butter, margarine, spread or oil) in small bowl. Microwave at MEDIUM (50%) 1 minute; stir. If necessary, microwave at MEDIUM an additional 15 seconds at a time, stirring after each heating until chips are melted when stirred.

Jolly Peanut Butter Gingerbread Cookies

MAKES ABOUT 6 DOZEN COOKIES

1⅔ cups (10-ounce package) REESE'S Peanut Butter Chips

¾ cup (1½ sticks) butter or margarine, softened

1 cup packed light brown sugar

1 cup dark corn syrup

2 eggs

5 cups all-purpose flour

1 teaspoon baking soda

½ teaspoon ground cinnamon

¼ teaspoon ground ginger

¼ teaspoon salt

1 Place peanut butter chips in small microwave-safe bowl. Microwave at MEDIUM (50%) 1 minute; stir. If necessary, microwave at MEDIUM an additional 15 seconds at a time, stirring after each heating, until chips are melted when stirred. Beat melted peanut butter chips and butter in large bowl until well blended. Add brown sugar, corn syrup and eggs; beat until fluffy.

2 Stir together flour, baking soda, cinnamon, ginger and salt. Add half of flour mixture to butter mixture; beat on low speed of mixer until smooth. With wooden spoon, stir in remaining flour mixture until well blended. Divide into thirds; wrap each in plastic wrap. Refrigerate at least 1 hour or until dough is firm enough to roll.

3 Heat oven to 325°F. On lightly floured surface, roll 1 dough portion at a time to ⅛-inch thickness; cut into holiday shapes with floured cookie cutters. Place on ungreased cookie sheet.

4 Bake 10 to 12 minutes or until set and lightly browned. Cool slightly; remove from cookie sheet to wire rack. Cool completely. Frost and decorate as desired.

Chocolate X and O Cookies

MAKES ABOUT 5 DOZEN COOKIES

⅔	cup butter or margarine, softened
1	cup sugar
2	teaspoons vanilla extract
2	eggs
2	tablespoons light corn syrup
2½	cups all-purpose flour
½	cup HERSHEY'S Cocoa
½	teaspoon baking soda
¼	teaspoon salt
	Decorating icing

1 Beat butter, sugar and vanilla in large bowl on medium speed of mixer until fluffy. Add eggs; beat well. Beat in corn syrup.

2 Combine flour, cocoa, baking soda and salt; gradually add to butter mixture, beating until well blended. Cover; refrigerate until dough is firm enough to handle.

3 Heat oven to 350°F. Shape dough into X and O shapes.* Place on ungreased cookie sheet.

4 Bake 5 minutes or until set. Remove from cookie sheet to wire rack. Cool completely. Decorate as desired with icing.

To shape X's: Shape rounded teaspoons of dough into 3-inch logs. Place 1 log on cookie sheet; press lightly in center. Place another 3-inch log on top of first one, forming X shape. To shape O's: Shape rounded teaspoon dough into 5-inch logs. Connect ends, pressing lightly, forming O shape.

Hanukkah Coin Cookies

1   cup (2 sticks) butter or margarine, softened

1   cup sugar

1   egg

1   teaspoon vanilla extract

1¾   cups all-purpose flour

½   cup HERSHEY'S Cocoa

1½   teaspoons baking powder

½   teaspoon salt

BUTTERCREAM FROSTING (recipe follows)

1 Beat butter, sugar, egg and vanilla in large bowl until well blended. Stir together flour, cocoa, baking powder and salt; gradually add to butter mixture, beating until well blended. Divide dough in half; place each half on separate sheet of wax paper.

2 Shape each portion into log, about 7 inches long. Wrap each log in wax paper or plastic wrap. Refrigerate until firm, at least 8 hours.

3 Heat oven to 325°F. Cut logs into ¼-inch-thick slices. Place on ungreased cookie sheet.

4 Bake 8 to 10 minutes or until set. Cool slightly; remove from cookie sheet to wire rack. Cool completely. Prepare BUTTERCREAM FROSTING; spread over tops of cookies.

Buttercream Frosting

¼   cup (½ stick) butter, softened

1½   cups powdered sugar

1   to 2 tablespoons milk

½   teaspoon vanilla extract

Yellow food color

Beat butter until creamy. Gradually add powdered sugar and milk to butter, beating to desired consistency. Stir in vanilla and food color.

MAKES ABOUT 1 CUP FROSTING

Chocolate Swirl Lollipop Cookies

MAKES ABOUT 24 COOKIES

½ cup (1 stick) butter or margarine, softened

1 cup sugar

2 eggs

1 teaspoon orange extract

1 teaspoon vanilla extract

2¼ cups all-purpose flour, divided

½ teaspoon baking soda

½ teaspoon salt

¼ teaspoon freshly grated orange peel

Few drops red and yellow food color (optional)

2 sections (½ ounce each) HERSHEY'S Unsweetened Chocolate Baking Bar, melted

About 24 wooden popsicle sticks

1 Beat butter and sugar in large bowl until blended. Add eggs and extracts; beat until light and fluffy. Gradually add 1¼ cups flour, blending until smooth. Stir in remaining 1 cup flour, baking soda and salt until mixture is well blended.

2 Place half of batter in medium bowl; stir in orange peel. Stir in food color, if desired. Melt chocolate as directed on package; stir into remaining half of batter. Cover; refrigerate both mixtures until firm enough to roll.

3 With rolling pin or fingers, between 2 pieces of wax paper, roll chocolate and orange mixtures each into 10×8-inch rectangle. Remove wax paper; place orange mixture on top of chocolate. Starting on longest side, roll up doughs tightly, forming into 12-inch roll; wrap in plastic wrap. Refrigerate until firm.

4 Heat oven to 350°F. Remove plastic wrap from roll; cut into ½-inch-wide slices. Place on cookie sheet at least 3 inches apart. Insert popsicle stick into each cookie.

5 Bake 8 to 10 minutes or until cookie is almost set. Cool slightly; remove from cookie sheet to wire rack. Cool completely. Decorate and tie with ribbon, if desired.

Fudge-Filled Butter Cookies

MAKES ABOUT 4 DOZEN COOKIES

- 1 cup (2 sticks) butter or margarine, softened
- ½ cup sugar
- 1 teaspoon vanilla extract
- 2 egg yolks
- 2 cups all-purpose flour
- ½ teaspoon baking powder
- ¼ teaspoon salt
- ½ cup HERSHEY'S Mini Chips Semi-Sweet Chocolate
- FUDGE FILLING (recipe follows)

1 Beat butter, sugar, vanilla and egg yolks in large bowl until light and fluffy. Stir together flour, baking powder and salt; gradually add to butter mixture, beating until well blended. Stir in small chocolate chips.

2 Refrigerate about 30 minutes or until firm enough to handle. Meanwhile, prepare FUDGE FILLING. Heat oven to 350°F.

3 Shape dough into 1-inch balls; place 2 inches apart on ungreased cookie sheet. Press thumb in center of each to make indentation; fill with scant teaspoonful filling.

4 Bake 10 to 12 minutes or until light brown around edges. Cool slightly; remove from cookie sheet to wire rack. Cool completely. Store, covered, in refrigerator.

Fudge Filling

- 1 tablespoon sugar
- 2 teaspoons cornstarch
- ½ cup whipping cream
- 1 egg yolk
- ½ cup HERSHEY'S Mini Chips Semi-Sweet Chocolate
- ½ teaspoon vanilla extract

Stir together sugar and cornstarch in small saucepan; gradually stir in whipping cream. Cook over low heat, stirring constantly, until smooth and thick. Beat egg yolk slightly in small bowl. Stir about 2 tablespoons hot mixture into yolk. Return to saucepan, stirring until blended. Cook, stirring constantly, just until mixture comes to a boil. Remove from heat; add small chocolate chips and vanilla, stirring until chips are melted. Cool.

Chocolate-Cherry Slice 'n' Bake Cookies

MAKES ABOUT 7½ DOZEN COOKIES

¾   cup (1½ sticks) butter or margarine, softened

1   cup sugar

1   egg

1½   teaspoons vanilla extract

2¼   cups all-purpose flour

2   teaspoons baking powder

½   teaspoon salt

¼   cup finely chopped maraschino cherries

½   teaspoon almond extract

Red food color

⅓   cup HERSHEY'S Cocoa

¼   teaspoon baking soda

4   teaspoons water

COCOA ALMOND GLAZE (recipe follows, optional)

1 Beat butter, sugar, egg and vanilla in large bowl until fluffy. Stir together flour, baking powder and salt; gradually add to butter mixture, beating until mixture forms a smooth dough. Remove 1¼ cups dough to medium bowl; blend in cherries, almond extract and about 6 drops food color.

2 Stir together cocoa and baking soda. Add with water to remaining dough; blend until smooth. Divide chocolate dough in half; roll each half between two sheets of wax paper, forming 12×4½-inch rectangle. Remove top sheet of wax paper. Divide cherry mixture in half; with floured hands, shape each half into 12-inch roll. Place one roll in center of each rectangle; wrap chocolate dough around roll, forming one large roll. Wrap each roll in plastic wrap. Refrigerate about 6 hours or until firm.

3 Heat oven to 350°F.

4 Cut rolls into ¼-inch-thick slices; place on ungreased cookie sheet. Bake 7 minutes or until set. Cool 1 minute; remove from cookie sheet to wire rack. Cool completely. Decorate cookies with COCOA ALMOND GLAZE, if desired.

Cocoa Almond Glaze

2   tablespoons butter or margarine

2   tablespoons HERSHEY'S Cocoa

2   tablespoons water

1   cup powdered sugar

⅛   teaspoon almond extract

Melt butter in small saucepan over low heat. Add cocoa and water; stir constantly until mixture thickens. Do not boil. Remove from heat. Add powdered sugar and almond extract, beating until smooth and of desired consistency. Add additional water, ½ teaspoon at a time, if needed.

MAKES ABOUT ½ CUP GLAZE

Peanut Butter Cut-Out Cookies

MAKES ABOUT 3 DOZEN COOKIES

½   cup (1 stick) butter or margarine

1   cup REESE'S Peanut Butter Chips

⅔   cup packed light brown sugar

1   egg

¾   teaspoon vanilla extract

1⅓   cups all-purpose flour

¾   teaspoon baking soda

½   cup finely chopped pecans

CHOCOLATE CHIP GLAZE (recipe follows)

1 Place butter and peanut butter chips in medium saucepan; cook over low heat, stirring constantly, until melted. Pour into large bowl; add brown sugar, egg and vanilla, beating until well blended. Stir in flour, baking soda and pecans, blending well. Refrigerate 15 to 20 minutes or until firm enough to roll.

2 Heat oven to 350°F.

3 Roll a small portion of dough at a time on lightly floured board, or between 2 pieces of wax paper, to ¼-inch thickness. (Keep remaining dough in refrigerator.) With cookie cutters, cut dough into desired shapes; place on ungreased cookie sheets.

4 Bake 7 to 8 minutes or until almost set (do not overbake). Cool 1 minute; remove from cookie sheets to wire racks. Cool completely. Drizzle CHOCOLATE CHIP GLAZE onto each cookie; allow to set.

Chocolate Chip Glaze: Place 1 cup HERSHEY'S SPECIAL DARK Chocolate Chips or HERSHEY'S Semi-Sweet Chocolate Chips and 1 tablespoon shortening (do not use butter, margarine, spread or oil) in small microwave-safe bowl. Microwave at MEDIUM (50%) 1 minute; stir. If necessary, microwave at MEDIUM an additional 15 seconds at a time, stirring after each heating, just until chips are melted and mixture is smooth.

KISSES Macaroon Cookies

MAKES ABOUT 4 DOZEN COOKIES

- ⅓ cup butter or margarine, softened
- 1 package (3 ounces) cream cheese, softened
- ¾ cup sugar
- 1 egg yolk
- 2 teaspoons almond extract
- 2 teaspoons orange juice
- 1¼ cups all-purpose flour
- 2 teaspoons baking powder
- ¼ teaspoon salt
- 5 cups MOUNDS Sweetened Coconut Flakes, divided
- 48 HERSHEY'S KISSESBRAND Milk Chocolates

1 Beat butter, cream cheese and sugar with electric mixer on medium speed in large bowl until well blended. Add egg yolk, almond extract and orange juice; beat well. Stir together flour, baking powder and salt; gradually add to butter mixture. Stir in 3 cups coconut. Cover; refrigerate 1 hour or until firm enough to handle. Meanwhile, remove wrappers from chocolates.

2 Heat oven to 350°F.

3 Shape dough into 1-inch balls; roll in remaining 2 cups coconut. Place on ungreased cookie sheet.

4 Bake 10 to 12 minutes or until lightly browned. Immediately press chocolate piece into center of each cookie. Cool 1 minute. Carefully remove to wire rack and cool completely.

candies & gifts

REESE'S Peanut Butter Bark

MAKES ABOUT 1 POUND CANDY

2	packages (4 ounces each) HERSHEY'S Semi-Sweet Chocolate Baking Bars, broken into pieces
1⅔	cups (10-ounce package) REESE'S Peanut Butter Chips
1	tablespoon shortening (do not use butter, margarine, spread or oil)
½	cup roasted peanuts or toasted almonds,* coarsely chopped

To toast almonds: Heat oven to 350°F. Spread almonds in thin layer in shallow baking pan. Bake 8 to 10 minutes, stirring occasionally, until light golden brown; cool.

1 Cover tray with wax paper.

2 Place chocolate in medium microwave-safe bowl. Microwave at MEDIUM (50%) 1 minute; stir. If necessary, microwave at MEDIUM an additional 30 seconds at a time, stirring after each heating, until chocolate is melted and smooth when stirred.

3 Immediately place peanut butter chips and shortening in second microwave-safe bowl. Microwave at MEDIUM 1 minute; stir. If necessary, microwave at MEDIUM an additional 30 seconds at a time, stirring after each heating, until chips are melted and mixture is smooth when stirred; stir in peanuts.

4 Alternately spoon above mixtures onto prepared tray; swirl with knife for marbled effect. Cover; refrigerate until firm. Break into pieces.

Chocolate and Orange Meltaways

MAKES 2 DOZEN PIECES

2 cups (12-ounce package) HERSHEY'S Premier White Chips, divided

½ cup (1 stick) unsalted butter (do not substitute margarine)

⅓ cup whipping cream

1½ teaspoons orange extract

CHOCOLATE COATING (recipe follows)

½ teaspoon shortening (do not use butter, margarine, spread or oil)

1 Line tray with wax paper. Reserve 2 tablespoons white chips.

2 Combine butter and whipping cream in medium saucepan; cook over low heat, stirring constantly until mixture comes to a full rolling boil. Remove from heat; immediately add remaining white chips. Stir with whisk until smooth. Add orange extract; blend well.

3 Refrigerate until firm enough to handle, about 2 hours. Taking small amount of mixture at a time, shape into 1-inch balls. Place on prepared tray; refrigerate until firm, about 1½ hours. Prepare CHOCOLATE COATING. Place one candy onto fork; dip into coating, covering completely and allowing excess to drip off. Place candies onto prepared tray. Repeat with remaining candies. Refrigerate until coating is set, about 1 hour.

4 Place reserved 2 tablespoons white chips and shortening in small microwave-safe bowl. Microwave at MEDIUM (50%) 30 seconds; stir. If necessary, microwave at MEDIUM an additional 10 seconds or until mixture is smooth when stirred. With fork, lightly drizzle over coated candies; refrigerate until set, about 20 minutes. Cover; store in refrigerator.

Chocolate Coating: Place 2 packages (4 ounces each) HERSHEY'S Semi-Sweet Chocolate Baking Bars, broken into pieces, and 1 teaspoon shortening (do not use butter, margarine, spread or oil) in medium microwave-safe bowl. Microwave at MEDIUM (50%) 2 minutes; stir. If necessary, microwave at MEDIUM an additional 15 seconds at a time, stirring after each heating, until chocolate is melted and mixture is smooth when stirred. Cool slightly. (If chocolate is too hot, it will not coat candy.)

Peanut Butter Chip Brittle

MAKES ABOUT 2 POUNDS BRITTLE

- 1⅔ cups (10-ounce package) REESE'S Peanut Butter Chips, divided
- 1½ cups (3 sticks) butter or margarine
- 1¾ cups sugar
- 3 tablespoons light corn syrup
- 3 tablespoons water

1 Butter 15½ × 10½ × 1-inch jelly-roll pan.* Sprinkle 1 cup peanut butter chips evenly onto bottom of prepared pan; set aside.

2 Melt butter in heavy 2½-quart saucepan; stir in sugar, corn syrup and water. Cook over medium heat, stirring constantly, until mixture reaches 300°F on candy thermometer. (This should take 30 to 35 minutes. Bulb of thermometer should not rest on bottom of saucepan.)

3 Remove from heat. Immediately spread mixture in prepared pan; sprinkle with remaining ⅔ cup peanut butter chips. Cool completely. Remove from pan. Break into pieces. Store in tightly covered container in cool, dry place.

For thicker brittle, use a 13 × 9-inch pan.

Spicy Cocoa Glazed Pecans

MAKES 1½ CUPS COATED PECANS

¼   **cup plus 2 tablespoons sugar, divided**

1   **cup warm water**

1½   **cups pecan halves or pieces**

1   **tablespoon HERSHEY'S Cocoa**

3   **to 4 teaspoons chili powder**

⅛   **to ¼ teaspoon cayenne pepper**

1 Heat oven to 350°F. Lightly spray shallow baking pan with vegetable cooking spray.

2 Stir together ¼ cup sugar and warm water, stirring until sugar dissolves. Add pecans; let soak 10 minutes. Drain water and discard.

3 Stir together remaining 2 tablespoons sugar, cocoa, chili powder and cayenne pepper in medium bowl. Add pecans; toss until all cocoa mixture coats pecans. Spread coated pecans on prepared pan.

4 Bake 10 to 15 minutes or until pecans start to glisten and appear dry. Stir occasionally while baking. Cool completely. Store in cool, dry place. Serve as a snack with beverages or sprinkle in salads.

Toffee Scones Mix

MAKES 2 DOZEN SCONES

3¼   cups all-purpose flour

½   cup sugar

1   tablespoon plus 1 teaspoon baking powder

¼   teaspoon salt

1⅓   cups (8-ounce package) HEATH BITS 'O BRICKLE Toffee Bits

½   cup toasted chopped walnuts*

BAKING INSTRUCTIONS (recipe follows)

To toast walnuts: Heat oven to 350°F. Spread walnuts in thin layer in shallow baking pan. Bake 8 to 10 minutes, stirring occasionally. Cool.

1 Stir together flour, sugar, baking powder, salt, toffee bits and walnuts. Place in 1-quart heavy-duty resealable plastic food storage bag. Press out air; seal.

2 Place toffee baking mix bag in decorative gift bag or container. Attach BAKING INSTRUCTIONS.

Baking Instructions:

1 Heat oven to 375°F. Lightly grease 2 baking sheets.

2 Empty contents of toffee baking mix into large bowl. Stir 2 cups (1 pint) whipping cream into mixture, stirring just until ingredients are moistened.

3 Turn mixture out onto lightly floured surface. Knead gently until soft dough forms (about 2 minutes). Divide dough into three equal balls. One ball at a time, flatten into 7-inch circle; cut into 8 triangles. Transfer triangles to prepared baking sheets, spacing 2 inches apart. Brush with melted butter and sprinkle with sugar.

4 Bake 15 to 20 minutes or until lightly browned. Serve warm or cool.

Marshmallow Marble-Top Fudge

MAKES ABOUT 5 DOZEN PIECES OR 2 POUNDS

- **2** cups miniature marshmallows
- **2** tablespoons butter or margarine
- **2** cups (12-ounce package) HERSHEY'S SPECIAL DARK Chocolate Chips or HERSHEY'S Semi-Sweet Chocolate Chips
- **1** can (14 ounces) sweetened condensed milk (not evaporated milk)
- **1** teaspoon vanilla extract
- Dash salt
- **½** to 1 cup chopped nuts

1 Line 8- or 9-inch square pan with foil. Place marshmallows and butter in medium microwave-safe bowl; set aside.

2 Place chocolate chips, sweetened condensed milk, vanilla and salt in large microwave-safe bowl. Microwave at HIGH (100%) 1 minute; stir. If necessary, microwave at HIGH an additional 15 seconds at a time, stirring after each heating, until chips are melted and mixture is smooth. Stir in nuts. Spread evenly in prepared pan.

3 Microwave marshmallows and butter at HIGH 30 seconds; stir. If necessary, microwave at HIGH an additional 30 seconds or until marshmallows are melted and mixture is smooth when stirred. Immediately spoon onto fudge. With table knife or metal spatula, swirl through fudge.

4 Refrigerate 2 hours or until firm. Remove fudge from pan; peel off foil. Cut into squares using wet knife. Store loosely covered at room temperature.

Note: For best results, do not double this recipe.

Tip: Fudge will cut even easier if refrigerated overnight.

Peanut Butter Fudge Balls

¼ cup (½ stick) butter

½ cup REESE'S Creamy Peanut Butter

¼ cup milk

3⅔ cups powdered sugar

1 teaspoon vanilla extract

3 cups finely chopped peanuts

1½ cups HERSHEY'S SPECIAL DARK Chocolate Chips or HERSHEY'S Semi-Sweet Chocolate Chips

1½ teaspoons shortening (do not use butter, margarine, spread or oil)

1 Line 8- or 9-inch square pan with foil; butter foil.

2 Cook butter, peanut butter and milk in large saucepan over very low heat, stirring constantly, until mixture is melted. With wooden spoon gradually beat in powdered sugar and vanilla. Remove from heat; pour into prepared pan. Cool completely. (Mixture will appear dry, but softens when rolled into balls.)

3 Line two trays with wax paper. Spread chopped peanuts on one tray; set aside. Roll peanut butter mixture into ¾-inch balls and place on second tray. If necessary, refrigerate peanut butter balls until firm enough to handle easily for coating.

4 Place chocolate chips and shortening in medium microwave-safe bowl. Microwave at MEDIUM (50%) 1 minute; stir. If necessary, microwave at MEDIUM an additional 15 seconds at a time, stirring after each heating, until chips are melted and mixture is smooth when stirred. Cool slightly.

5 Dip peanut butter balls completely into chocolate mixture, one at a time, with fork. Gently tap fork on side of bowl to remove excess chocolate. Immediately roll in chopped peanuts; gently reshape if necessary. Place candy balls into small paper candy cups or return to wax paper-lined tray. Refrigerate until firm, about 20 minutes. Store in cool, dry place.

Note: Recipe can be doubled.

Filled Chocolate Meringues

MAKES 2 DOZEN MERINGUES

2	egg whites, at room temperature
¼	teaspoon cream of tartar
	Dash salt
½	cup sugar
½	teaspoon vanilla extract
2	tablespoons HERSHEY'S Cocoa

CHOCOLATE-CHEESE FILLING (recipe follows)

Raspberries and mint leaves for garnish

1 Heat oven to 275°F. Place parchment paper on cookie sheets.

2 Beat egg whites with cream of tartar and salt in medium bowl until soft peaks form. Beat in sugar, 1 tablespoon at a time, until stiff, glossy peaks form. Fold in vanilla. Sift cocoa over top of egg white mixture; gently fold in cocoa until combined. Drop by tablespoonfuls onto parchment paper. With back of small spoon, make indentation in center of each mound.

3 Bake 45 minutes or until meringue turns a light cream color and feels dry to the touch. Cool slightly; carefully peel meringues off parchment paper; cool completely on wire racks. To serve, spoon or pipe about 2 teaspoons CHOCOLATE-CHEESE FILLING into center of each meringue. Garnish each with a raspberry and a mint leaf.

Chocolate-Cheese Filling:

Combine 1 cup part-skim ricotta cheese, 2 tablespoons HERSHEY'S Cocoa, 1 tablespoon sugar and ½ teaspoon vanilla extract in food processor; blend until smooth. Cover; refrigerate. Makes 1 cup filling.

Double Peanut Clusters

1⅔ cups (10-ounce package) REESE'S Peanut Butter Chips

1 tablespoon shortening (do not use butter, margarine, spread or oil)

2 cups salted peanuts

1 Line cookie sheet with wax paper.

2 Place peanut butter chips and shortening in large microwave-safe bowl. Microwave at MEDIUM (50%) 1½ minutes; stir until chips are melted and mixture is smooth. If necessary, microwave an additional 30 seconds until chips are melted when stirred. Stir in peanuts.

3 Drop by rounded teaspoons onto prepared cookie sheet. (Mixture may also be dropped into small paper candy cups.) Cool until set. Store in cool, ..dry place.

Butterscotch Nut Clusters: Follow above directions, substituting 1¾ cups (11-ounce package) HERSHEY'S Butterscotch Chips for peanut butter chips.

127

Jingle Bells Chocolate Pretzels

MAKES ABOUT 24 COATED PRETZELS

1 cup HERSHEY'S SPECIAL DARK Chocolate Chips or HERSHEY'S Semi-Sweet Chocolate Chips

1 cup HERSHEY'S Premier White Chips, divided

1 tablespoon plus ½ teaspoon shortening (do not use butter, margarine, spread or oil), divided

About 24 salted or unsalted pretzels (3×2 inches)

1 Cover tray or cookie sheet with wax paper.

2 Place chocolate chips, ⅔ cup white chips and 1 tablespoon shortening in medium microwave-safe bowl. Microwave at MEDIUM (50%) 1 minute; stir. Microwave at MEDIUM an additional 1 to 2 minutes, stirring every 30 seconds, until chips are melted when stirred.

3 Using fork, dip each pretzel into chocolate mixture; tap fork on side of bowl to remove excess chocolate. Place coated pretzels on prepared tray.

4 Place remaining ⅓ cup white chips and remaining ½ teaspoon shortening in small microwave-safe bowl. Microwave at MEDIUM 15 to 30 seconds or until chips are melted when stirred. Using tines of fork, drizzle chip mixture across pretzels.

Refrigerate until coating is set. Store in airtight container in cool, dry place.

White Dipped Pretzels: Cover tray with wax paper. Place 2 cups (12-ounce package) HERSHEY'S Premier White Chips and 2 tablespoons shortening (do not use butter, margarine, spread or oil) in medium microwave-safe bowl. Microwave at MEDIUM 1 to 2 minutes or until chips are melted when stirred. Dip pretzels as directed above. Place ¼ cup HERSHEY'S SPECIAL DARK Chocolate Chips or HERSHEY'S Semi-Sweet Chocolate Chips and ¼ teaspoon shortening (do not use butter, margarine, spread or oil) in small microwave-safe bowl. Microwave at MEDIUM 30 seconds to 1 minute or until chips are melted when stirred. Drizzle melted chocolate across pretzels, using tines of fork. Refrigerate and store as directed above.

Chocolate Truffles

- ¾ cup (1½ sticks) butter
- ¾ cup HERSHEY'S Cocoa
- 1 can (14 ounces) sweetened condensed milk (not evaporated milk)
- 1 tablespoon vanilla extract
- Cocoa or powdered sugar

1 Melt butter in heavy saucepan over low heat. Add cocoa; stir until smooth. Add sweetened condensed milk; increase heat to medium. Cook, stirring constantly, about 4 minutes or until mixture has pudding-like consistency and is smooth and glossy.

2 Remove from heat; stir in vanilla. Cover; refrigerate 3 to 4 hours or until firm. Shape into 1¼-inch balls; roll in cocoa or powdered sugar. Refrigerate until firm, 1 to 2 hours. Store, covered, in refrigerator.

Nut Truffles: Add ¾ cup coarsely chopped toasted pecans to chocolate mixture when adding vanilla. (To toast pecans: Heat oven to 375°F. Spread ¾ cup pecan halves or pieces in single layer in ungreased shallow baking pan. Bake 5 to 7 minutes, stirring occasionally. Cool before chopping.)

Rum Nut Truffles: Decrease vanilla to 1 teaspoon. Stir in 2 to 3 tablespoons rum or 1 teaspoon rum extract and nuts.

Espresso Truffles: Decrease vanilla to 1 teaspoon. Stir in 1¼ teaspoons powdered instant espresso or instant coffee when adding vanilla. Roll balls in cocoa or chopped nuts.

Nut-Coated Truffles: Roll balls in chopped nuts.

Chocolate Buttercream Cherry Candies

MAKES ABOUT 48 CANDIES

About 48 maraschino cherries with stems, well drained

¼ cup (½ stick) butter, softened

2 cups powdered sugar

¼ cup HERSHEY'S Cocoa or HERSHEY'S SPECIAL DARK Cocoa

1 to 2 tablespoons milk, divided

½ teaspoon vanilla extract

¼ teaspoon almond extract

WHITE CHIP COATING (recipe follows)

CHOCOLATE CHIP DRIZZLE (recipe follows)

1 Cover tray with wax paper. Lightly press cherries between layers of paper towels to remove excess moisture.

2 Beat butter, powdered sugar, cocoa and 1 tablespoon milk in small bowl until well blended; stir in vanilla and almond extract. If necessary, add remaining milk, 1 teaspoon at a time, until mixture will hold together but is not wet.

3 Mold scant teaspoon mixture around each cherry, covering completely; place on prepared tray. Cover; refrigerate 3 hours or until firm.

4 Prepare WHITE CHIP COATING. Holding each cherry by stem, dip into coating. Place on tray; refrigerate until firm.

5 About 1 hour before serving, prepare CHOCOLATE CHIP DRIZZLE; with tines of fork drizzle randomly over candies. Refrigerate until drizzle is firm. Store in refrigerator.

White Chip Coating: Place 2 cups (12-ounce package) HERSHEY'S Premier White Chips in small microwave-safe bowl; drizzle with 2 tablespoons vegetable oil. Microwave at MEDIUM (50%) 1 minute; stir. If necessary, microwave at MEDIUM an additional 15 seconds at a time, stirring after each heating just until chips are melted and mixture is smooth. If mixture thickens while coating, microwave at MEDIUM 15 seconds; stir until smooth.

Chocolate Chip Drizzle: Place ¼ cup HERSHEY'S SPECIAL DARK Chocolate Chips or HERSHEY'S Semi-Sweet Chocolate Chips and ¼ teaspoon shortening (do not use butter, margarine, spread or oil) in another small microwave-safe bowl. Microwave at MEDIUM (50%) 30 seconds to 1 minute; stir until chips are melted and mixture is smooth.

Gumdrop Bark

MAKES ABOUT 1 POUND CANDY

About ¼ cup red spice gumdrops*

About ¼ cup green spice gumdrops*

2 cups (12-ounce package) HERSHEY'S Premier White Chips

*Amounts and gumdrop flavors can vary according to your own preference.

1 Line cookie sheet with wax paper. Cut gumdrops into slices about ¼-inch thick; set aside.

2 Place white chips in medium microwave-safe bowl. Microwave at MEDIUM (50%) 1 minute; stir. Continue microwaving at MEDIUM in 15-second increments, stirring after each heating, until chips are melted and smooth when stirred.

3 Pour melted chips onto prepared cookie sheet; spread to about ½-inch thickness. Gently tap cookie sheet on countertop to even out thickness of melted chips. Sprinkle gumdrop slices over surface. Repeat tapping cookie sheet on counter until candy is desired thickness.

4 Refrigerate about 30 minutes or until firm. Break into pieces. Store in cool, dry place.

Rich Cocoa Fudge

3 cups sugar

⅔ cup HERSHEY'S Cocoa or HERSHEY'S SPECIAL DARK Cocoa

⅛ teaspoon salt

1½ cups milk

¼ cup (½ stick) butter

1 teaspoon vanilla extract

1 Line 8- or 9-inch square pan with foil, extending foil over edges of pan. Butter foil.

2 Stir together sugar, cocoa and salt in heavy 4-quart saucepan; stir in milk. Cook over medium heat, stirring constantly, until mixture comes to full rolling boil. Boil, without stirring, until mixture reaches 234°F on candy thermometer or until small amount of mixture dropped into very cold water forms a soft ball which flattens when removed from water. (Bulb of candy thermometer should not rest on bottom of saucepan.) Remove from heat.

3 Add butter and vanilla. DO NOT STIR. Cool at room temperature to 110°F (lukewarm). Beat with wooden spoon until fudge thickens and just begins to lose some of its gloss. Quickly spread in prepared pan; cool completely. Cut into squares. Store in tightly covered container at room temperature.

Nutty Rich Cocoa Fudge: Beat cooked fudge as directed. Immediately stir in 1 cup chopped almonds, pecans or walnuts and quickly spread in prepared pan.

Marshmallow Nut Cocoa Fudge: Increase cocoa to ¾ cup. Cook fudge as directed. Add 1 cup marshmallow crème with butter and vanilla. DO NOT STIR. Cool to 110°F (lukewarm). Beat 8 minutes; stir in 1 cup chopped nuts. Pour into prepared pan. (Fudge does not set until poured into pan.)

Notes: For best results, do not double this recipe. This is one of our most requested recipes, but also one of our most difficult. The directions must be followed exactly. Beat too little and the fudge is too soft. Beat too long and it becomes hard and sugary.

Classic MINI KISSES Cookie Mix (Cookie Mix in a Jar)

MAKES 1 JAR MIX

2¼ cups all-purpose flour

⅔ cup granulated sugar

1 teaspoon baking soda

½ teaspoon salt

1½ cups HERSHEY'S MINI KISSES BRAND Milk Chocolates, divided

⅔ cup packed light brown sugar

BAKING INSTRUCTIONS (recipe follows)

1 Stir together flour, granulated sugar, baking soda and salt. Transfer mixture to clean 1-quart (4 cups) glass jar with lid; pack down into bottom of jar.

2 Layer with 1 cup chocolate pieces and brown sugar.* Top with remaining ½ cup chocolates; close jar. Attach card with BAKING INSTRUCTIONS.

To increase shelf life of mix, wrap brown sugar in plastic wrap and press into place.

Classic MINI KISSES Cookies

1 jar Classic MINI KISSES BRAND Cookie Mix

1 cup (2 sticks) butter, softened and cut into pieces

1 teaspoon vanilla extract

2 eggs, lightly beaten

Baking Instructions:

1 Heat oven to 375°F.

2 Spoon contents of jar into large bowl; stir to break up any lumps. Add butter and vanilla; stir until crumbly mixture forms. Add eggs; stir to form smooth, very stiff dough. Drop by heaping teaspoons onto ungreased cookie sheet.

3 Bake 8 to 10 minutes or until lightly browned. Cool slightly; remove from cookie sheet to wire rack. Cool completely.

MAKES 36 COOKIES

Tip: For best results, use cookie mix within 4 weeks of assembly.

Chocolate Mint Squares

MAKES ABOUT 4 DOZEN PIECES

6	**tablespoons butter (no substitutes)**
½	**cup HERSHEY'S Cocoa**
2	**cups powdered sugar**
3	**tablespoons plus 1 teaspoon milk, divided**
1	**teaspoon vanilla extract**
	MINT FILLING (recipe follows)

1 Line 8-inch square pan with foil, extending foil over edges of pan.

2 Melt butter in small saucepan over low heat; add cocoa. Cook, stirring constantly, just until mixture is smooth. Remove from heat; add powdered sugar, 3 tablespoons milk and vanilla. Cook over low heat, stirring constantly, until mixture is glossy. Spread half of mixture into prepared pan. Refrigerate.

3 Meanwhile, prepare MINT FILLING; spread filling over chocolate layer. Refrigerate 10 minutes.

4 To remaining chocolate mixture in saucepan, add remaining 1 teaspoon milk. Cook over low heat, stirring constantly, until smooth. Spread quickly over filling. Refrigerate until firm. Use foil to lift candy out of pan; peel off foil. Cut candy into squares. Store in tightly covered container in refrigerator.

Mint Filling

1	**package (3 ounces) cream cheese, softened**
2	**cups powdered sugar**
½	**teaspoon vanilla extract**
¼	**teaspoon peppermint extract**
3	**to 5 drops green food color**
	Milk

Beat cream cheese, powdered sugar, vanilla, peppermint extract and food color in small bowl until smooth. Add 2 to 3 teaspoons milk, if needed, for spreading consistency.

kid-friendly munchies & snacks

Peanut Butter and Milk Chocolate Chip Cattails

MAKES 12 TO 14 COATED PRETZELS

- **1** cup HERSHEY'S Milk Chocolate Chips, divided
- **1** cup REESE'S Peanut Butter Chips, divided
- **2** teaspoons shortening (do not use butter, margarine, spread or oil)
- **12** to 14 pretzel rods

1 Stir together milk chocolate chips and peanut butter chips. Place sheet of wax paper on tray or counter top. Finely chop 1 cup chip mixture in food processor or by hand; place on wax paper. Line tray or cookie sheet with wax paper.

2 Place remaining 1 cup chip mixture and shortening in narrow deep microwave-safe bowl. Microwave at MEDIUM (50%) 1 minute; stir. If necessary, microwave additional 15 seconds at a time, stirring after each heating, until chips are melted and mixture is smooth when stirred.

3 Spoon chocolate-peanut butter mixture over about ¾ of pretzel rod; gently shake off excess. Holding pretzel by uncoated end, roll in chopped chips, pressing chips into chocolate. Place on prepared tray. Refrigerate 30 minutes or until set. Store coated pretzels in cool, dry place.

Variation: Melt 1 cup milk chocolate chips and 1 cup peanut butter chips with 4 teaspoons shortening; dip small pretzels into mixture.

Ice Cream Sandwiches

MAKES ABOUT 12 (4-INCH) ICE CREAM SANDWICHES

½	cup shortening
1	cup sugar
1	egg
1	teaspoon vanilla extract
1⅔	cups all-purpose flour
⅓	cup HERSHEY'S Cocoa
½	teaspoon baking soda
½	teaspoon salt
¼	cup milk

Desired flavor ice cream, slightly softened

Assorted chopped HERSHEY'S, REESE'S or HEATH baking pieces, crushed peppermints or other small candies (optional)

1 Beat shortening, sugar, egg and vanilla in large bowl until well blended. Stir together flour, cocoa, baking soda and salt; add alternately with milk to sugar mixture, beating until well blended. Cover; refrigerate about 1 hour.

2 Heat oven to 375°F. Drop batter by heaping tablespoons onto ungreased cookie sheet. With palm of hand or bottom of glass, flatten each cookie into 2¾-inch circle, about ¼-inch thick. Bake 8 to 10 minutes or until almost set. Cool 1 minute; remove from cookie sheet to wire rack. Cool completely.

3 Place scoop of ice cream on flat side of 1 cookie; spread evenly with spatula. Top with another cookie, pressing together lightly; repeat with remaining cookies. Roll ice cream edges in chopped baking pieces or candies, if desired. Wrap individually in foil; freeze until firm.

Cinnamon Chips Gems

MAKES 4 DOZEN COOKIES

- 1 cup (2 sticks) butter or margarine, softened
- 2 packages (3 ounces each) cream cheese, softened
- 2 cups all-purpose flour
- ½ cup sugar
- ⅓ cup ground toasted almonds
- 2 eggs
- 1 can (14 ounces) sweetened condensed milk (not evaporated milk)
- 1 teaspoon vanilla extract
- 1⅓ cups HERSHEY'S Cinnamon Chips, divided

1 Beat butter and cream cheese in large bowl until well blended; stir in flour, sugar and almonds. Cover; refrigerate about 1 hour.

2 Divide dough into 4 equal parts. Shape each part into 12 smooth balls. Place each ball in small muffin cup (1¾ inches in diameter); press evenly on bottom and up side of each cup.

3 Heat oven to 375°F. Beat eggs in small bowl. Add sweetened condensed milk and vanilla; mix well. Place 7 cinnamon chips in bottom of each cookie shell; fill a generous ¾ full with sweetened condensed milk mixture.

4 Bake 18 to 20 minutes or until tops are puffed and just beginning to turn golden brown. Cool 3 minutes. Sprinkle about 15 chips on top of each cookie. Cool completely in pan on wire rack. Remove from pan using small metal spatula or sharp knife. Store tightly covered at room temperature.

Chocolate-Covered Banana Pops

MAKES 9 POPS

3   ripe large bananas

9   wooden popsicle sticks

2   cups (12-ounce package) HERSHEY'S SPECIAL DARK Chocolate Chips or HERSHEY'S Semi-Sweet Chocolate Chips

2   tablespoons shortening (do not use butter, margarine, spread or oil)

1½   cups coarsely chopped unsalted, roasted peanuts

1 Peel bananas; cut each into thirds. Insert a wooden stick into each banana piece; place on wax paper-covered tray. Cover; freeze until firm.

2 Place chocolate chips and shortening in medium microwave-safe bowl. Microwave at MEDIUM (50%) 1½ to 2 minutes or until chocolate is melted and mixture is smooth when stirred.

3 Remove bananas from freezer just before dipping. Dip each piece into warm chocolate, covering completely; allow excess to drip off. Immediately roll in peanuts. Cover; return to freezer. Serve frozen.

Variation: HERSHEY'S Milk Chocolate Chips or HERSHEY'S Mini Chips Semi-Sweet Chocolate may be substituted for HERSHEY'S SPECIAL DARK Chocolate Chips or HERSHEY'S Semi-Sweet Chocolate Chips.

COOKIES, CANDIES & SNACKS

Boo Bites

MAKES ABOUT 4 DOZEN PIECES

¼	cup (½ stick) butter or margarine
30	large marshmallows or 3 cups miniature marshmallows
¼	cup light corn syrup
½	cup REESE'S Creamy Peanut Butter
⅓	cup HERSHEY'S SPECIAL DARK Chocolate Chips or HERSHEY'S Semi-Sweet Chocolate Chips
4½	cups crisp rice cereal

1 Line cookie sheet with wax paper.

2 Melt butter in large saucepan over low heat. Add marshmallows. Cook, stirring constantly, until marshmallows are melted. Remove from heat. Add corn syrup; stir until well blended. Add peanut butter and chocolate chips; stir until chips are melted and mixture is well blended.

3 Add cereal; stir until evenly coated. Cool slightly. With wet hands, shape mixture into 1½-inch balls; place balls on prepared cookie sheet. Cool completely. Store in tightly covered container in cool, dry place.

Cookie Pizza

MAKES ABOUT 12 SLICES

- **1** package (18 ounces) refrigerated sugar cookie dough
- **12** assorted **HERSHEY'S MINIATURES** Chocolate Bars, unwrapped
- **¼** cup **HERSHEY'S SPECIAL DARK** Chocolate Chips, **HERSHEY'S** Semi-Sweet Chocolate Chips or **HERSHEY'S** Milk Chocolate Chips
- **¼** cup **REESE'S Peanut Butter Chips**
- **¼** cup **HERSHEY'S Premier White Chips**
- **1** bag (10½ ounces) miniature marshmallows
- **¼** cup **HERSHEY'S MILK DUDS Candy** made with chocolate and caramels

1 Heat oven to 350°F. Press cookie dough evenly onto 12-inch pizza pan. Bake 15 to 17 minutes or until lightly browned. Meanwhile, break or cut chocolate bars into about ¼-inch pieces.

2 Remove cookie from oven. Evenly sprinkle surface with chocolate chips, peanut butter chips, white chips and chocolate bar pieces. Cover "toppings" with marshmallows. Sprinkle surface with chocolate-covered caramel candies. Return to oven; bake additional 5 minutes or until marshmallows are puffed and lightly browned. Cool. Cut into triangles.

Cauldron Dipped Apples

MAKES 8 TO 10 DIPPED APPLES

8 to 10 medium apples, stems removed

8 to 10 wooden ice cream sticks

PEANUT BUTTER SUGAR (recipe follows)

2 cups (12-ounce package) HERSHEY'S SPECIAL DARK Chocolate Chips or HERSHEY'S Semi-Sweet Chocolate Chips

¼ cup shortening (do not use butter, margarine, spread or oil)

⅔ cup REESE'S Creamy Peanut Butter

⅔ cup powdered sugar

1 Line tray with wax paper. Wash and dry apples; insert wooden stick into stem end of each apple.

2 Prepare PEANUT BUTTER SUGAR.

3 Melt chocolate chips and shortening in medium saucepan over low heat. Remove from heat. Add peanut butter; stir until melted and smooth. With whisk, blend in powdered sugar.

4 Dip apples into chocolate mixture; twirl gently to remove excess. Sprinkle PEANUT BUTTER SUGAR over apples. Place on prepared tray. Refrigerate until coating is firm. Store in refrigerator.

Peanut Butter Sugar

3 tablespoons REESE'S Creamy Peanut Butter

⅓ cup powdered sugar

1 tablespoon granulated sugar

Combine all ingredients in small bowl.

MAKES ABOUT ⅔ CUP

Drizzled Party Popcorn

MAKES ABOUT 8 CUPS POPCORN

- 8 cups popped popcorn
- ½ cup HERSHEY'S Milk Chocolate Chips
- 2 teaspoons shortening (do not use butter, margarine, spread or oil), divided
- ½ cup REESE'S Peanut Butter Chips

1 Line cookie sheet or jelly-roll pan with wax paper. Spread popcorn in thin layer on prepared pan.

2 Place milk chocolate chips and 1 teaspoon shortening in microwave-safe bowl. Microwave at MEDIUM (50%) 30 seconds; stir. If necessary, microwave at MEDIUM an additional 10 seconds at a time, stirring after each heating, until chips are melted and smooth when stirred. Drizzle over popcorn.

3 Place peanut butter chips and remaining 1 teaspoon shortening in separate microwave-safe bowl. Microwave at MEDIUM 30 seconds; stir. If necessary, microwave at MEDIUM an additional 10 seconds at a time, stirring after each heating, until chips are melted and smooth when stirred. Drizzle over popcorn.

4 Allow drizzle to set up at room temperature or refrigerate about 10 minutes or until firm. Break popcorn into pieces.

Notes: Popcorn is best eaten the same day as prepared, but it can be stored in an airtight container. Recipe amounts can be changed to match your personal preferences.

Greeting Card Cookies

MAKES ABOUT 12 COOKIES

½ cup (1 stick) butter or margarine, softened

¾ cup sugar

1 egg

1 teaspoon vanilla extract

1½ cups all-purpose flour

⅓ cup HERSHEY'S Cocoa

½ teaspoon baking powder

½ teaspoon baking soda

¼ teaspoon salt

DECORATIVE FROSTING (recipe follows)

1 Beat butter, sugar, egg and vanilla in large bowl until fluffy. Stir together flour, cocoa, baking powder, baking soda and salt; add to butter mixture, blending well. Refrigerate about 1 hour or until firm enough to roll. Cut cardboard rectangle for pattern, 2½×4 inches; wrap in plastic wrap.

2 Heat oven to 350°F. Lightly grease cookie sheet or line with parchment paper. On lightly floured board or between two pieces of wax paper, roll out half of dough to ¼-inch thickness. For each cookie, place pattern on dough; cut through dough around pattern with sharp paring knife. (Save dough trimmings and reroll for remaining cookies.) Carefully place cutouts on prepared cookie sheet.

3 Bake 8 to 10 minutes or until set. Cool 1 minute on cookie sheet. (If cookies have lost their shape, trim irregular edges while cookies are still hot.) Carefully transfer to wire rack. Repeat procedure with remaining dough.

4 Prepare DECORATIVE FROSTING; spoon into pastry bag fitted with decorating tip. Pipe names or greetings onto cookies; decorate as desired.

Decorative Frosting

3 cups powdered sugar

⅓ cup shortening

2 to 3 tablespoons milk

Food color (optional)

Beat powdered sugar and shortening in small bowl; gradually add milk, beating until smooth and slightly thickened. Cover until ready to use. If desired, divide frosting into two or more bowls; tint each a different color with food color.

S'more for Me

MAKES 12 DESSERTS

1	package (6-serving size) vanilla cook & serve pudding and pie filling mix*
3	cups milk
8	(1.55 ounces each) HERSHEY'S Milk Chocolate Bars, broken into pieces
12	single-serve graham cracker crumb crusts
1½	cups miniature marshmallows
12	HERSHEY'S MINIATURES Milk Chocolate Bars

Do not use instant pudding mix.

1 Stir together pudding mix and milk in a saucepan. Cook over medium heat, stirring constantly, until mixture comes to a full boil; remove from heat.

2 Add chocolate bar pieces; stir until chocolate is melted and mixture is smooth.

3 Spoon about ⅓ cup pudding mixture into each individual graham crust. Press plastic wrap onto pudding surface; refrigerate until ready to serve. (This step may be done up to 3 days before serving.)

To Serve: **Heat oven to 350°F. Remove plastic wrap. Place 10 to 12 miniature marshmallows on surface of each pudding. Bake 10 minutes or until marshmallows are puffed and lightly toasted. Place on serving plate; gently place unwrapped miniature chocolate bar on top of marshmallows. Serve immediately.

Dessert will be hot, but should cool sufficiently by the time it gets to the table. Pudding will be warm and the chocolate bar will be slightly melted.

Marbled Peanut Butter Brownies

MAKES ABOUT 36 BROWNIES

2	packages (3 ounces each) cream cheese, softened
½	cup REESE'S Creamy Peanut Butter
2¼	cups sugar, divided
4	eggs
2	tablespoons milk
1	cup (2 sticks) butter or margarine
2	teaspoons vanilla extract
¾	cup HERSHEY'S Cocoa
1¼	cups all-purpose flour
½	teaspoon baking powder
¼	teaspoon salt
1	cup HERSHEY'S Milk Chocolate Chips or 1 cup HERSHEY'S MINI KISSESBRAND Milk Chocolates

1 Heat oven to 350°F. Grease 13×9×2-inch pan.

2 Prepare peanut butter filling by beating cream cheese, peanut butter, ¼ cup sugar, 1 egg and milk.

3 Melt butter in large microwave-safe bowl at HIGH (100%) 2 to 2½ minutes or until melted. Stir in remaining 2 cups sugar and vanilla. Add remaining 3 eggs, 1 at a time, beating well with spoon after each addition. Add cocoa; beat until well blended. Add flour, baking powder and salt; beat well. Stir in chocolate chips.

4 Remove 1 cup batter; set aside. Pour remaining batter into prepared pan. Spread peanut butter filling over surface. Drop reserved chocolate batter by teaspoons over filling. Using knife, gently swirl through top layers for marbled effect.

5 Bake 35 to 40 minutes or until wooden pick inserted in center comes out almost clean. Cool completely in pan on wire rack; cut into bars.

HERSHEY'S Easy Chocolate Cracker Snacks

MAKES ABOUT 5½ DOZEN CRACKERS

1⅔ cups (10-ounce package) HERSHEY'S Mint Chocolate Chips*

2 cups (12-ounce package) HERSHEY'S SPECIAL DARK Chocolate Chips or HERSHEY'S Semi-Sweet Chocolate Chips

2 tablespoons shortening (do not use butter, margarine, spread or oil)

60 to 70 round buttery crackers (about one-half 1-pound box)

2 cups (11.5-ounce package) HERSHEY'S Milk Chocolate Chips and ¼ teaspoon pure peppermint extract can be substituted for mint chocolate chips.

1 Line several trays or cookie sheets with wax paper.

2 Place mint chocolate chips, chocolate chips and shortening in large microwave-safe bowl. Microwave at MEDIUM (50%) 1 minute; stir. Continue heating 30 seconds at a time, stirring after each heating, until chips are melted and mixture is smooth when stirred.

3 Drop crackers into chocolate mixture one at a time. Using tongs, push cracker into chocolate so that it is covered completely. (If chocolate begins to thicken, reheat 10 to 20 seconds in microwave.) Remove from chocolate, tapping lightly on edge of bowl to remove excess chocolate. Place on prepared tray. Refrigerate until chocolate hardens, about 20 minutes. For best results, store tightly covered in refrigerator.

Peanut Butter and Milk Chocolate: Use 1⅔ cups (10-ounce package) REESE'S Peanut Butter Chips, 2 cups (11.5-ounce package) HERSHEY'S Milk Chocolate Chips and 2 tablespoons shortening. Proceed as directed.

White Chip and Toffee: Melt 2 bags (12 ounces each) HERSHEY'S Premier White Chips and 2 tablespoons shortening. Dip crackers; before coating hardens sprinkle with HEATH BITS 'O BRICKLE Toffee Bits.

Easter Nest Cookies

MAKES ABOUT 3½ DOZEN COOKIES

1½	cups all-purpose flour
1	teaspoon baking powder
½	teaspoon salt
¾	cup (1½ sticks) butter
2	cups miniature marshmallows
½	cup sugar
1	egg white
1	teaspoon vanilla extract
½	teaspoon almond extract
3¾	cups MOUNDS Sweetened Coconut Flakes, divided
	JOLLY RANCHER Jelly Beans
	HERSHEY'S Candy-Coated Milk Chocolate Eggs

1 Heat oven to 375°F.

2 Stir together flour, baking powder and salt; set aside. Place butter and marshmallows in microwave-safe bowl. Microwave at HIGH (100%) 1 to 1½ minutes or just until mixture melts when stirred. Beat sugar, egg white, vanilla and almond extract in separate bowl; add melted butter mixture, beating until light and fluffy. Gradually add flour mixture, beating until blended. Stir in 2 cups coconut.

3 Shape dough into 1-inch balls; roll balls in remaining 1¾ cups coconut, tinting coconut, if desired.* Place balls on ungreased cookie sheet. Press thumb into center of each ball, creating shallow depression.

4 Bake 8 to 10 minutes or just until lightly browned. Place 1 to 3 jelly beans and milk chocolate eggs in center of each cookie. Transfer to wire rack; cool completely.

To Tint Coconut: Place ¾ teaspoon water and a few drops food color in small bowl; stir in 1¾ cups coconut. Toss with fork until evenly tinted; cover tightly.

REESE'S Haystacks

1⅔ cups (10-ounce package) REESE'S Peanut Butter Chips

1   tablespoon shortening (do not use butter, margarine, spread or oil)

2½   cups (5-ounce can) chow mein noodles

1 Line tray with wax paper.

2 Place peanut butter chips and shortening in medium microwave-safe bowl. Microwave at MEDIUM (50%) 1 minute; stir. If necessary, microwave at MEDIUM an additional 15 seconds at a time, stirring after each heating, just until chips are melted and mixture is smooth when stirred. Immediately add chow mein noodles; stir to coat.

3 Drop mixture by heaping teaspoons onto prepared tray or into paper candy cups. Let stand until firm. If necessary, cover and refrigerate several minutes until firm. Store in tightly covered container.

contents

CAKES & CHEESECAKES

167

180

196

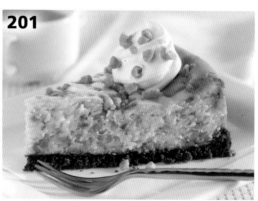
201

easy layer cakes

European Mocha Fudge Cake

MAKES 10 TO 12 SERVINGS

1 ¼	cups (2 ½ sticks) butter or margarine
¾	cup HERSHEY'S SPECIAL DARK Cocoa
4	eggs
¼	teaspoon salt
1	teaspoon vanilla extract
2	cups sugar
1	cup all-purpose flour
1	cup finely chopped pecans
	CREAMY COFFEE FILLING (recipe follows)
	Chocolate curls (optional)

1 Heat oven to 350°F. Butter bottom and sides of two 9-inch round baking pans. Line bottoms with wax paper; butter paper.

2 Melt butter in small saucepan; remove from heat. Add cocoa, stirring until blended; cool slightly. Beat eggs in large bowl until foamy; add salt and vanilla. Gradually add sugar, beating well. Add cooled chocolate mixture; blend thoroughly. Fold in flour. Stir in pecans. Pour mixture into prepared pans.

3 Bake 20 to 25 minutes or until wooden pick inserted in center comes out clean. Do not overbake. Cool 5 minutes; remove from pans to wire racks. Carefully peel off paper. Cool completely. Spread CREAMY COFFEE FILLING between layers, over top and sides of cake. Garnish with chocolate curls, if desired. Refrigerate 1 hour or longer before serving. Cover leftover cake; store in refrigerator.

Creamy Coffee Filling

1 ½	cups cold whipping cream
⅓	cup packed light brown sugar
2	teaspoons powdered instant coffee

Combine all ingredients; stir until instant coffee is almost dissolved. Beat until stiff.

MAKES ABOUT 3 CUPS FILLING

Make-Ahead Directions: Cooled cake may be wrapped and frozen up to 4 weeks; thaw, wrapped, before filling and frosting.

Sour Cream Chocolate Cake

MAKES 8 TO 10 SERVINGS

½   cup HERSHEY'S Cocoa

½   cup hot water

½   cup (1 stick) butter or margarine, softened

1   cup granulated sugar

½   cup packed light brown sugar

1½   teaspoons vanilla extract

3   eggs

1¾   cups all-purpose flour

1½   teaspoons baking powder

1   teaspoon baking soda

1   teaspoon salt

1   cup (8 ounces) dairy sour cream

    QUICK FUDGE FROSTING (recipe follows)

1 Heat oven to 350°F. Grease and flour two 9-inch round baking pans.

2 Combine cocoa and water in small bowl; stir until smooth. Set aside.

3 Beat butter in large bowl until creamy. Add granulated sugar, brown sugar and vanilla; beat until fluffy. Add eggs; beat well. Stir in cocoa mixture. Stir together flour, baking powder, baking soda and salt; add alternately with sour cream to butter mixture, beating just until blended. Pour batter into prepared pans.

4 Bake 30 to 35 minutes or until wooden pick inserted in center comes out clean. Cool 15 minutes; remove from pans to wire racks. Cool completely. Frost with QUICK FUDGE FROSTING.

Quick Fudge Frosting

6   to 7 tablespoons light cream or evaporated milk

⅓   cup butter or margarine, softened

3   cups powdered sugar

6   tablespoons HERSHEY'S Cocoa

⅛   teaspoon salt

1   teaspoon vanilla extract

1 Heat cream in small saucepan until bubbles form around edge of pan; remove from heat and set aside.

2 Beat butter in medium bowl until creamy. Stir together powdered sugar, cocoa and salt; add alternately with cream to butter, beating to spreading consistency. Stir in vanilla.

MAKES ABOUT 2 CUPS FROSTING

Peanut Cream-Filled "Perfectly Chocolate" Chocolate Cake

MAKES 12 SERVINGS

- 2 cups granulated sugar
- 1¾ cups all-purpose flour
- ¾ cup HERSHEY'S Cocoa
- 1½ teaspoons baking powder
- 1½ teaspoons baking soda
- 1 teaspoon salt
- 2 eggs
- 1 cup milk
- ½ cup vegetable oil
- 2 teaspoons vanilla extract
- 1 cup boiling water
- PEANUT BUTTER CREAM (recipe follows)
- COCOA GLAZE (recipe follows)

1 Heat oven to 350°F. Grease and flour two 9-inch round pans.

2 Combine dry ingredients in large bowl. Add eggs, milk, oil and vanilla. Beat 2 minutes on medium speed. Stir in boiling water (batter will be thin). Pour into pans.

3 Bake 30 to 35 minutes. Cool 10 minutes; remove from pans to wire racks. Cool completely.

4 Prepare and spread half of PEANUT BUTTER CREAM between layers; spread remainder on top. Refrigerate 30 minutes. Drizzle with COCOA GLAZE. Store, covered, in refrigerator.

Peanut Butter Cream: Cook ½ cup milk and 1⅔ cups (10-ounce package) REESE'S Peanut Butter Chips over low heat, stirring constantly, until smooth. Cool to room temperature (about 30 minutes). Gradually fold in 3 cups (8-ounce tub) thawed frozen non-dairy whipped topping. Makes about 3½ cups.

Cocoa Glaze: Melt 1½ tablespoons butter; add 1½ tablespoons HERSHEY'S Cocoa and 1½ tablespoons water, stirring until thickened. Remove from heat. Gradually add ½ cup powdered sugar; whisk until smooth. Stir in ¼ teaspoon vanilla extract. Makes about ⅓ cup glaze.

HERSHEY'S "Especially Dark" Chocolate Cake

MAKES 10 TO 12 SERVINGS

- 2 **cups sugar**
- 1¾ **cups all-purpose flour**
- ¾ **cup HERSHEY'S SPECIAL DARK Cocoa**
- 1½ **teaspoons baking powder**
- 1½ **teaspoons baking soda**
- 1 **teaspoon salt**
- 2 **eggs**
- 1 **cup milk**
- ½ **cup vegetable oil**
- 2 **teaspoons vanilla extract**
- 1 **cup boiling water**
- **"ESPECIALLY DARK" CHOCOLATE FROSTING (recipe follows)**

1 Heat oven to 350°F. Grease and flour two 9-inch round baking pans.

2 Stir together sugar, flour, cocoa, baking powder, baking soda and salt in large bowl. Add eggs, milk, oil and vanilla; beat with electric mixer on medium speed for 2 minutes. Stir in boiling water (batter will be thin). Pour batter into prepared pans.

3 Bake 30 to 35 minutes or until wooden pick inserted in center comes out clean. Cool 10 minutes; remove from pans to wire racks. Cool completely. Frost with "ESPECIALLY DARK" CHOCOLATE FROSTING.

"Especially Dark" Chocolate Frosting

- ½ **cup (1 stick) butter or margarine**
- ⅔ **cup HERSHEY'S SPECIAL DARK Cocoa**
- 3 **cups powdered sugar**
- ⅓ **cup milk**
- 1 **teaspoon vanilla extract**

Melt butter. Stir in cocoa. Alternately add powdered sugar and milk, beating to spreading consistency. Add small amount additional milk, if needed. Stir in vanilla.

MAKES 2 CUPS FROSTING

Collector's Cocoa Cake

MAKES 8 TO 10 SERVINGS

- ¾ cup (1½ sticks) butter or margarine, softened
- 1¾ cups sugar
- 2 eggs
- 1 teaspoon vanilla extract
- 2 cups all-purpose flour
- ¾ cup HERSHEY'S Cocoa or HERSHEY'S SPECIAL DARK Cocoa
- 1¼ teaspoons baking soda
- ½ teaspoon salt
- 1⅓ cups water
- FLUFFY PEANUT BUTTER FROSTING or ONE-BOWL BUTTERCREAM FROSTING (recipes follow)

1 Heat oven to 350°F. Grease and flour two 8- or 9-inch round baking pans.

2 Beat butter and sugar in large bowl until fluffy. Add eggs and vanilla; beat 1 minute on medium speed of mixer. Stir together flour, cocoa, baking soda and salt; add alternately with water to butter mixture, beating until well blended. Pour batter into prepared pans.

3 Bake 35 to 40 minutes for 8-inch layers; 30 to 35 minutes for 9-inch layers or until wooden pick inserted in center comes out clean. Cool 10 minutes; remove from pans to wire racks. Cool completely.

4 Frost with FLUFFY PEANUT BUTTER FROSTING or ONE-BOWL BUTTERCREAM FROSTING.

Fluffy Peanut Butter Frosting

- 1 cup milk
- ¼ cup all-purpose flour
- 1 cup sugar
- ½ cup REESE'S Creamy Peanut Butter
- ½ cup shortening
- 1 teaspoon vanilla extract
- Dash salt

1 Gradually stir milk into flour in small saucepan. Cook over low heat, stirring constantly, until very thick. Transfer to medium bowl; press plastic wrap directly on surface. Cool to room temperature, about ½ hour.

2 Add sugar, peanut butter, shortening, vanilla and salt. Beat on high speed of mixer until frosting becomes fluffy and sugar is completely dissolved.

MAKES ABOUT 3 CUPS FROSTING

One-Bowl Buttercream Frosting

- 6 tablespoons butter or margarine, softened
- 2⅔ cups powdered sugar
- ½ cup HERSHEY'S Cocoa or HERSHEY'S SPECIAL DARK Cocoa
- ⅓ cup milk
- 1 teaspoon vanilla extract

Beat butter in medium bowl. Add powdered sugar and cocoa alternately with milk; beat to spreading consistency (additional milk may be needed). Stir in vanilla.

MAKES ABOUT 2 CUPS FROSTING

German Chocolate Cake

MAKES 10 TO 12 SERVINGS

¼	cup HERSHEY'S Cocoa
½	cup boiling water
1	cup (2 sticks) plus 3 tablespoons butter or margarine, softened
2¼	cups sugar
1	teaspoon vanilla extract
4	eggs
2	cups all-purpose flour
1	teaspoon baking soda
½	teaspoon salt
1	cup buttermilk or sour milk*
	COCONUT PECAN FROSTING (recipe follows)
	Pecan halves (optional)

*To sour milk: Use 1 tablespoon white vinegar plus milk to equal 1 cup.

Cool 5 minutes; remove from pans. Cool completely on wire rack. Prepare COCONUT PECAN FROSTING; spread between layers and over top. Garnish with pecan halves, if desired.

1 Heat oven to 350°F. Grease and flour three 9-inch round baking pans. Combine cocoa and water in small bowl; stir until smooth. Set aside to cool.

2 Beat butter, sugar and vanilla in large bowl until fluffy. Add eggs, one at a time, beating well after each addition. Stir together flour, baking soda and salt; add alternately with chocolate mixture and buttermilk to butter mixture. Mix only until smooth. Pour batter into prepared pans.

3 Bake 25 to 30 minutes or until top springs back when touched lightly.

Coconut Pecan Frosting

1	can (14 ounces) sweetened condensed milk (not evaporated milk)
3	egg yolks, slightly beaten
½	cup (1 stick) butter or margarine
1	teaspoon vanilla extract
1⅓	cups MOUNDS Sweetened Coconut Flakes
1	cup chopped pecans

1 Place sweetened condensed milk, egg yolks and butter in medium saucepan. Cook over low heat, stirring constantly, until mixture is thickened and bubbly.

2 Remove from heat; stir in vanilla, coconut and pecans. Cool to room temperature.

MAKES ABOUT 2⅔ CUPS FROSTING

Autumn Peanutty Carrot Cake

MAKES 10 TO 12 SERVINGS

3	eggs
¾	cup vegetable oil
1	teaspoon vanilla extract
1½	cups all-purpose flour
¾	cup granulated sugar
½	cup packed light brown sugar
2	teaspoons ground cinnamon
1¼	teaspoons baking soda
2	cups grated carrots
1⅔	cups (10-ounce package) REESE'S Peanut Butter Chips
½	cup chopped walnuts
	CREAM CHEESE FROSTING (recipe follows)

1 Heat oven to 350°F. Grease and flour two 8-inch round baking pans.

2 Beat eggs, oil and vanilla in large bowl. Stir together flour, granulated sugar, brown sugar, cinnamon and baking soda; add to egg mixture and blend well. Stir in carrots, peanut butter chips and walnuts; pour into prepared pans.

3 Bake 30 to 35 minutes or until wooden pick inserted in center comes out clean. Cool 10 minutes; remove from pans to wire rack. Cool completely. Frost with CREAM CHEESE FROSTING. Cover; refrigerate leftover cake.

Cream Cheese Frosting: Beat 2 packages (3 ounces each) softened cream cheese and ½ cup (1 stick) softened butter until smooth. Gradually add 4 cups powdered sugar and 2 teaspoons vanilla extract, beating until smooth.

HERSHEY'S "Perfectly Chocolate" Chocolate Cake

MAKES 10 TO 12 SERVINGS

- **2** cups sugar
- **1¾** cups all-purpose flour
- **¾** cup HERSHEY'S Cocoa
- **1½** teaspoons baking powder
- **1½** teaspoons baking soda
- **1** teaspoon salt
- **2** eggs
- **1** cup milk
- **½** cup vegetable oil
- **2** teaspoons vanilla extract
- **1** cup boiling water
- **"PERFECTLY CHOCOLATE" CHOCOLATE FROSTING (recipe follows)**

1 Heat oven to 350°F. Grease and flour two 9-inch round baking pans.

2 Stir together sugar, flour, cocoa, baking powder, baking soda and salt in large bowl. Add eggs, milk, oil and vanilla; beat on medium speed of mixer 2 minutes. Stir in boiling water (batter will be thin). Pour batter evenly into prepared pans.

3 Bake 30 to 35 minutes or until wooden pick inserted into center comes out clean. Cool 10 minutes; remove from pans to wire racks. Cool completely. Frost with "PERFECTLY CHOCOLATE" CHOCOLATE FROSTING.

One-Pan Cake: Grease and flour 13×9×2-inch baking pan. Heat oven to 350°F. Pour batter into prepared pan. Bake 35 to 40 minutes. Cool completely. Frost.

Three Layer Cake: Grease and flour three 8-inch round baking pans. Heat oven to 350°F. Pour batter into prepared pans. Bake 30 to 35 minutes. Cool 10 minutes; remove from pans to wire racks. Cool completely. Frost.

Bundt Cake: Grease and flour 12-cup fluted tube pan. Heat oven to 350°F. Pour batter into prepared pan. Bake 50 to 55 minutes. Cool 15 minutes; remove from pan to wire rack. Cool completely. Frost.

Cupcakes: Line muffin cups (2½ inches in diameter) with paper bake cups. Heat oven to 350°F. Fill cups ⅔ full with batter. Bake 22 to 25 minutes. Cool completely. Frost. Makes about 30 cupcakes.

"Perfectly Chocolate" Chocolate Frosting

- **½** cup (1 stick) butter or margarine
- **⅔** cup HERSHEY'S Cocoa
- **3** cups powdered sugar
- **⅓** cup milk
- **1** teaspoon vanilla extract

Melt butter. Stir in cocoa. Alternately add powdered sugar and milk, beating to spreading consistency. Add small amount additional milk, if needed. Stir in vanilla.

MAKES ABOUT 2 CUPS FROSTING

Orange Cocoa Cake

½ cup HERSHEY'S Cocoa

½ cup boiling water

¼ cup (½ stick) butter or margarine, softened

¼ cup shortening

2 cups sugar

⅛ teaspoon salt

1 teaspoon vanilla extract

2 eggs

1½ teaspoons baking soda

1 cup buttermilk or sour milk*

1¾ cups all-purpose flour

3 tablespoons buttermilk or sour milk*

⅛ teaspoon baking soda

¾ teaspoon freshly grated orange peel

¼ teaspoon orange extract

ORANGE BUTTERCREAM FROSTING (recipe follows)

*To sour milk: Use 1 tablespoon vinegar plus milk to equal 1 cup; use ½ teaspoon vinegar plus milk to equal 3 tablespoons.

1 Heat oven to 350°F. Grease three 8- or 9-inch layer pans and line with wax paper; set aside.

2 Stir together cocoa and boiling water in small bowl until smooth; set aside. Beat butter, shortening, sugar, salt and vanilla in large bowl until fluffy. Add eggs; beat well. Stir 1½ teaspoons baking soda into 1 cup buttermilk; add alternately with flour to butter mixture.

3 Measure 1⅔ cups batter into small bowl. Stir in 3 tablespoons buttermilk, ⅛ teaspoon baking soda, the orange peel and orange extract; pour into one prepared pan. Stir cocoa mixture into remaining batter; divide evenly between remaining two prepared pans.

4 Bake 25 to 30 minutes or until wooden pick inserted in center comes out clean. Cool 10 minutes; remove from pans. Carefully peel off wax paper. Cool completely.

5 Place one chocolate layer on serving plate; spread with some of the ORANGE BUTTERCREAM FROSTING. Top with orange layer and spread with frosting. Top with remaining chocolate layer and frost entire cake.

Orange Buttercream Frosting

⅔ cup butter or margarine, softened

6 cups powdered sugar

2 teaspoons freshly grated orange peel

1½ teaspoons vanilla extract

4 to 6 tablespoons milk

Beat butter, 1 cup powdered sugar, the orange peel and vanilla in large bowl. Add remaining powdered sugar alternately with milk, beating to spreading consistency. If necessary, add additional milk, ½ teaspoon at a time, to get desired spreading consistency.

MAKES ABOUT 3 CUPS FROSTING

snack & coffee cakes

Orange Streusel Coffee Cake

MAKES 12 SERVINGS

COCOA STREUSEL (recipe follows)

¾ cup (1½ sticks) butter or margarine, softened

1 cup sugar

3 eggs

1 teaspoon vanilla extract

½ cup dairy sour cream

3 cups all-purpose flour

2 teaspoons baking powder

1 teaspoon baking soda

1 cup orange juice

2 teaspoons freshly grated orange peel

½ cup orange marmalade or apple jelly

1 Prepare COCOA STREUSEL. Heat oven to 350°F. Generously grease 12-cup fluted tube pan.

2 Beat butter and sugar in large bowl until well blended. Add eggs and vanilla; beat well. Add sour cream; beat until blended. Stir together flour, baking powder and baking soda; add alternately with orange juice to butter mixture, beating until well blended. Stir in orange peel.

3 Spread marmalade in bottom of prepared pan; sprinkle half of streusel over marmalade. Pour half of batter into pan, spreading evenly. Sprinkle remaining streusel over batter; spread remaining batter evenly over streusel.

4 Bake about 1 hour or until toothpick inserted near center of cake comes out clean. Loosen cake from side of pan with metal spatula; immediately invert onto serving plate. Serve warm or cool.

Cocoa Streusel: Stir together ⅔ cup packed light brown sugar, ½ cup chopped walnuts, ¼ cup HERSHEY'S Cocoa and ½ cup MOUNDS Sweetened Coconut Flakes, if desired.

HERSHEY'S SPECIAL DARK
Snack Cake Medley

MAKES 12 TO 16 SERVINGS

CREAM CHEESE FILLING (recipe follows)

- 3 cups all-purpose flour
- 2 cups sugar
- ⅔ cup HERSHEY'S Cocoa
- 2 teaspoons baking soda
- 1 teaspoon salt
- 2 cups water
- ⅔ cup vegetable oil
- 2 eggs
- 2 tablespoons white vinegar
- 2 teaspoons vanilla extract
- ½ cup HERSHEY'S SPECIAL DARK Chocolate Chips
- ½ cup MOUNDS Sweetened Coconut Flakes
- ½ cup chopped nuts

1 Heat oven to 350°F. Grease and flour 13×9×2-inch baking pan. Prepare CREAM CHEESE FILLING; set aside.

2 Stir together flour, sugar, cocoa, baking soda and salt in large bowl. Add water, oil, eggs, vinegar and vanilla; beat on medium speed of mixer 2 minutes or until well blended. Pour 3 cups batter into prepared pan. Gently drop CREAM CHEESE FILLING onto batter by heaping teaspoonfuls. Carefully spoon remaining batter over filling. Combine chocolate chips, coconut and nuts; sprinkle over top of batter.

3 Bake 50 to 55 minutes or until wooden pick inserted into cake center comes out almost clean and cake starts to crack slightly. Cool completely in pan on wire rack. Cover and store leftover cake in refrigerator.

Cream Cheese Filling

- ½ cup HERSHEY'S SPECIAL DARK Chocolate Chips
- 1 package (8 ounces) cream cheese, softened
- ⅓ cup sugar
- 1 egg
- ½ teaspoon vanilla extract

1 Place chocolate chips in small microwave-safe bowl. Microwave at MEDIUM (50%) 30 seconds; stir. If necessary, microwave an additional 10 seconds at a time, stirring after each heating, until chips are melted and smooth when stirred.

2 Beat cream cheese and sugar in medium bowl until well blended. Beat in egg and vanilla. Add melted chocolate, beating until well blended.

Cinnamon Chip Applesauce Coffee Cake

- 1 cup (2 sticks) butter or margarine, softened
- 1 cup granulated sugar
- 2 eggs
- ½ teaspoon vanilla extract
- ¾ cup applesauce
- 2½ cups all-purpose flour
- 1 teaspoon baking soda
- ½ teaspoon salt
- 1⅔ cups (10-ounce package) HERSHEY'S Cinnamon Chips
- 1 cup chopped pecans (optional)
- ¾ cup powdered sugar
- 1 to 2 tablespoons warm water

1 Heat oven to 350°F. Lightly grease 13×9×2-inch baking pan.

2 Beat butter and granulated sugar with electric mixer on medium speed in large bowl until well blended. Beat in eggs and vanilla. Mix in applesauce. Stir together flour, baking soda and salt; gradually add to butter mixture, beating until well blended. Stir in cinnamon chips and pecans, if desired. Spread in prepared pan.

3 Bake 30 to 35 minutes or until wooden pick inserted in center comes out clean. Cool in pan on wire rack. Sprinkle cake with powdered sugar or stir together ¾ cup powdered sugar and warm water to make smooth glaze; drizzle over cake. Serve at room temperature or while still slightly warm.

Fluted Cake: Grease and flour 12-cup fluted tube pan. Prepare batter as directed; pour into prepared pan. Bake 45 to 50 minutes or until wooden pick inserted in thickest part comes out clean. Cool 15 minutes; invert onto wire rack. Cool completely.

Cupcakes: Line 24 baking cups (2½ inches in diameter) with paper baking liners. Prepare batter as directed; divide evenly into prepared cups. Bake 15 to 18 minutes or until wooden pick inserted in center comes out clean. Cool completely.

Chocolate Streusel Coffee Cake

MAKES 12 TO 16 SERVINGS

CHOCOLATE STREUSEL (recipe follows)

½ cup (1 stick) butter or margarine, softened

1 cup sugar

3 eggs

1 container (8 ounces) dairy sour cream

1 teaspoon vanilla extract

2 cups all-purpose flour

1 teaspoon baking powder

1 teaspoon baking soda

¼ teaspoon salt

1 Heat oven to 350°F. Grease and flour 12-cup fluted tube pan. Prepare CHOCOLATE STREUSEL; set aside.

2 Beat butter and sugar in large bowl until fluffy. Add eggs; blend well on low speed of mixer. Stir in sour cream and vanilla. Combine flour, baking powder, baking soda and salt in separate bowl; add to batter. Blend well.

3 Sprinkle 1 cup CHOCOLATE STREUSEL into prepared pan. Spread ⅓ of the batter (about 1⅓ cups) in pan; sprinkle with half the remaining streusel (about 1 cup). Repeat layers, ending with batter on top.

4 Bake 50 to 55 minutes or until wooden pick inserted near center comes out clean. Cool 10 minutes; invert onto serving plate. Cool completely.

Chocolate Streusel

¾ cup packed light brown sugar

¼ cup all-purpose flour

¼ cup (½ stick) butter or margarine, softened

¾ cup chopped nuts

¾ cup HERSHEY'S Mini Chips Semi-Sweet Chocolate

Combine brown sugar, flour and butter in medium bowl until crumbly. Stir in nuts and small chocolate chips.

Chocolate Cake Fingers

MAKES 42 PIECES

1	cup granulated sugar
1	cup all-purpose flour
⅓	cup HERSHEY'S Cocoa
¾	teaspoon baking powder
¾	teaspoon baking soda
½	cup nonfat milk
¼	cup frozen egg substitute, thawed
¼	cup canola oil or vegetable oil
1	teaspoon vanilla extract
½	cup boiling water
	Powdered sugar
1	teaspoon freshly grated orange peel
1½	cups frozen light non-dairy whipped topping, thawed

1 Heat oven to 350°F. Line bottom of 13×9×2-inch baking pan with wax paper.

2 Stir together granulated sugar, flour, cocoa, baking powder and baking soda in large bowl. Add milk, egg substitute, oil and vanilla; beat on medium speed of mixer 2 minutes. Stir in boiling water (batter will be thin). Pour into prepared pan.

3 Bake 16 to 18 minutes or until wooden pick inserted in center comes out clean. With knife or metal spatula, loosen cake from edges of pan. Place clean, lint-free dish towel on wire rack; sprinkle lightly with powdered sugar. Invert cake on towel; peel off wax paper. Cool completely.

4 Invert cake, right side up, on cutting board. Cut cake into small rectangles (about 2×1 ¼ inches). Stir orange peel into whipped topping; spoon dollop on each piece of cake. Garnish as desired. Store ungarnished cake, covered, at room temperature.

Spicy Butterscotch Snack Cake

MAKES 12 TO 16 SERVINGS

- **1 cup (2 sticks) butter or margarine, softened**
- **1 cup sugar**
- **2 eggs**
- **½ teaspoon vanilla extract**
- **½ cup applesauce**
- **2½ cups all-purpose flour**
- **1½ to 2 teaspoons ground cinnamon**
- **1 teaspoon baking soda**
- **½ teaspoon salt**
- **1¾ cups (11-ounce package) HERSHEY'S Butterscotch Chips**
- **1 cup chopped pecans (optional)**
- **Powdered sugar or frozen whipped topping, thawed (optional)**

1 Heat oven to 350°F. Lightly grease 13×9×2-inch baking pan.

2 Beat butter and sugar in large bowl until fluffy. Add eggs and vanilla; beat well. Mix in applesauce. Stir together flour, cinnamon, baking soda and salt; gradually add to butter mixture, beating until well blended. Stir in butterscotch chips and pecans, if desired. Spread in prepared pan.

3 Bake 35 to 40 minutes or until wooden pick inserted in center comes out clean. Cool completely in pan on wire rack. Dust with powdered sugar or serve with whipped topping, if desired.

Milk Chocolate Tres Leche Cake

MAKES 12 TO 16 SERVINGS

½	cup (1 stick) butter, softened
1	cup sugar
5	eggs
2	teaspoons vanilla extract
1⅓	cups cake flour
⅓	cup HERSHEY'S Cocoa
1	teaspoon baking powder
½	teaspoon salt
	TRES LECHE GLAZE (recipe follows)
	CREAM TOPPING (recipe follows)

1 Heat oven to 350°F. Grease and flour 13×9×2-inch baking pan.

2 Beat butter in large bowl with electric mixer until light and fluffy. Gradually beat in sugar, continuing to beat about 1 minute. Add eggs, one at a time, beating well after each addition. Blend in vanilla. Stir together flour, cocoa, baking powder and salt. Gradually blend flour mixture into butter mixture, mixing just until blended. Pour batter into prepared pan.

3 Bake 20 to 25 minutes or until golden brown and wooden pick inserted in center comes out clean. Cool cake in pan on wire rack for 30 minutes. With skewer or fork, pierce the entire top of the cake. Prepare TRES LECHE GLAZE. Reserve 1½ cups glaze; pour remaining glaze over cake. Cover; refrigerate cake and reserved glaze overnight. (Cake should absorb most of the glaze and will be very wet.)

4 Prepare CREAM TOPPING. Spread topping over cake; refrigerate until ready to serve. To serve, pour 1 to 2 tablespoons of the reserved glaze onto bottom of each individual dessert dish. Place cake piece on this glaze. Garnish as desired. Cover; refrigerate leftovers.

Tres Leche Glaze: Stir together 2 cans (14 ounces each) sweetened condensed milk, 1 can (12 ounces) evaporated milk, 1 cup heavy cream and ¾ cup HERSHEY'S Chocolate Syrup in pitcher or large bowl.

Cream Topping: Beat 2 cups (1 pint) whipping cream, 1 cup sugar, ¼ cup HERSHEY'S Cocoa and 1 teaspoon vanilla extract in large mixing bowl until stiff.

White Chip and Macadamia Nut Coffee Cake

CRUMB TOPPING (recipe follows)

6 **tablespoons butter or margarine, softened**

¾ **cup granulated sugar**

¾ **cup packed light brown sugar**

2 **cups all-purpose flour**

2 **teaspoons baking powder**

½ **teaspoon ground cinnamon**

1¼ **cups milk**

1 **egg**

1 **teaspoon vanilla extract**

WHITE DRIZZLE (recipe follows)

1 Heat oven to 350°F. Grease and flour 13×9×2-inch baking pan. Prepare CRUMB TOPPING; set aside.

2 Beat butter, granulated sugar and brown sugar until well blended. Stir together flour, baking powder and cinnamon; beat into butter mixture. Gradually add milk, egg and vanilla, beating until thoroughly blended. Pour ½ batter into prepared pan; top with ½ CRUMB TOPPING. Gently spread remaining batter over topping. Sprinkle remaining topping over batter.

3 Bake 30 to 35 minutes or until wooden pick inserted in center comes out clean. Cool completely.

4 Prepare WHITE DRIZZLE; drizzle over cake.

Crumb Topping: Combine ⅔ cup packed light brown sugar, ½ cup all-purpose flour, 6 tablespoons firm butter or margarine, 1 cup HERSHEY'S Premier White Chips and ½ cup MAUNA LOA Macadamia Nut Baking Pieces in medium bowl. Mix until crumbly.

White Drizzle: Beat together ¾ cup powdered sugar, 2 to 3 teaspoons milk, 1 teaspoon softened butter and ¼ teaspoon vanilla extract. If necessary, stir in additional milk, ½ teaspoon at a time, until desired consistency.

Peanut Butter Coffee Cake

MAKES 12 TO 15 SERVINGS

1⅔	cups (10-ounce package) REESE'S Peanut Butter Chips
¾	cup REESE'S Creamy Peanut Butter
2¼	cups all-purpose flour
1½	cups packed light brown sugar
½	cup (1 stick) butter or margarine, softened
1	teaspoon baking powder
½	teaspoon baking soda
1	cup milk
3	eggs
1	teaspoon vanilla extract

1 Heat oven to 350°F. Grease bottom of 13×9×2-inch baking pan.

2 Place peanut butter chips and peanut butter in microwave-safe bowl. Microwave at MEDIUM (50%) 1 minute; stir. If necessary, microwave at MEDIUM an additional 15 seconds at a time, stirring after each heating, just until chips are melted when stirred.

3 Combine flour, brown sugar, butter and peanut butter chip mixture in large bowl. Beat on low speed of mixer until mixture resembles small crumbs; reserve 1 cup crumbs. To remaining crumb mixture, gradually blend in baking powder, baking soda, milk, eggs and vanilla; beat until well combined. Pour batter into prepared pan; sprinkle with reserved crumbs.

4 Bake 35 to 40 minutes or until wooden pick inserted in center comes out clean. Cool completely in pan on wire rack.

Nutty Toffee Coffee Cake

MAKES 12 TO 16 SERVINGS

- 1⅓ cups (8-ounce package) HEATH BITS 'O BRICKLE Toffee Bits, divided
- ⅓ cup plus ¾ cup packed light brown sugar, divided
- 2¼ cups all-purpose flour, divided
- 9 tablespoons butter or margarine, softened and divided
- ¾ cup granulated sugar
- 2 teaspoons baking powder
- ½ teaspoon ground cinnamon
- ¼ teaspoon salt
- 1¼ cups milk
- 1 egg
- 1 teaspoon vanilla extract
- ¾ cup chopped nuts

1 Heat oven to 350°F. Grease and flour 13×9×2-inch baking pan. Stir together ½ cup toffee bits, ⅓ cup brown sugar, ¼ cup flour and 3 tablespoons butter. Stir until crumbly; set aside.

2 Combine remaining 2 cups flour, granulated sugar, remaining ¾ cup brown sugar, remaining 6 tablespoons butter, baking powder, cinnamon and salt in large mixer bowl; mix until well blended. Gradually add milk, egg and vanilla, beating until thoroughly blended. Stir in remaining toffee bits and nuts. Spread batter in prepared pan.

3 Sprinkle reserved crumb topping over batter. Bake 30 to 35 minutes or until wooden pick inserted in center comes out clean. Serve warm or cool.

Chocolate Mini Cheesecakes

MAKES ABOUT 24 MINI CHEESECAKES

CHOCOLATE CRUMB CRUST (recipe follows)

½ cup HERSHEY'S Cocoa

¼ cup (½ stick) butter or margarine, melted

3 packages (8 ounces each) cream cheese, softened

1 can (14 ounces) sweetened condensed milk (not evaporated milk)

3 eggs

2 teaspoons vanilla extract

CHOCOLATE GLAZE (recipe follows)

1 Heat oven to 300°F. Line muffin cups (2½ inches in diameter) with paper bake cups or spray with vegetable cooking spray.* Press about 1 tablespoonful CHOCOLATE CRUMB CRUST mixture onto bottom of each cup.

2 Stir together cocoa and ¼ cup butter. Beat cream cheese until fluffy. Beat in cocoa mixture. Gradually beat in sweetened condensed milk. Beat in eggs and vanilla. Fill muffin cups with batter.

3 Bake 35 minutes or until set. Cool 15 minutes; remove from pan to wire rack. Cool completely. Refrigerate. Before serving, spread with CHOCOLATE GLAZE. Allow to set. Serve at room temperature.

If vegetable cooking spray is used, cool baked cheesecakes. Freeze 15 minutes; remove with narrow spatula.

Chocolate Crumb Crust: Stir together 1½ cups vanilla wafer crumbs (about 45 wafers, crushed), 6 tablespoons HERSHEY'S Cocoa, 6 tablespoons powdered sugar and 6 tablespoons melted butter or margarine in medium bowl.

Chocolate Glaze: Melt 1 cup HERSHEY'S SPECIAL DARK Chocolate Chips or HERSHEY'S Semi-Sweet Chocolate Chips with ½ cup whipping cream and ½ teaspoon vanilla extract in medium saucepan over low heat. Stir until smooth. Use immediately. Makes about 1 cup glaze.

Chocolate Chip Applesauce Snacking Cake

1⅓ cups all-purpose flour

1 cup granulated sugar

¾ teaspoon baking soda

¾ teaspoon salt

½ teaspoon ground cinnamon

¼ teaspoon baking powder

¼ teaspoon ground allspice

½ cup shortening

1 cup chunky applesauce

2 eggs

1 teaspoon vanilla extract

½ cup chopped pecans

½ cup HERSHEY'S SPECIAL DARK Chocolate Chips or HERSHEY'S Semi-Sweet Chocolate Chips

Powdered sugar (optional)

VANILLA FROSTING (recipe follows, optional)

CHOCOLATE DRIZZLE (recipe follows, optional)

1 Heat oven to 350°F. Grease and flour 9-inch square baking pan.

2 Combine flour, granulated sugar, baking soda, salt, cinnamon, baking powder and allspice in large bowl. Add shortening, applesauce, eggs and vanilla. Beat on low speed of mixer to combine; beat on medium speed 1 minute or until ingredients are well blended. Stir in pecans and chocolate chips; pour into prepared pan.

3 Bake 40 to 45 minutes or until wooden pick inserted in center comes out clean. Cool in pan on wire rack. Sprinkle with powdered sugar or spread VANILLA FROSTING on cake. Prepare CHOCOLATE DRIZZLE, if desired; drizzle over top of VANILLA FROSTING.

Vanilla Frosting: Beat 3 tablespoons softened butter or margarine in small bowl until fluffy. Add 1½ cups powdered sugar and ½ teaspoon vanilla extract alternately with 1 to 2 tablespoons milk, beating to spreading consistency. Makes about 1 cup frosting.

Chocolate Drizzle: Place ½ cup HERSHEY'S SPECIAL DARK Chocolate Chips or HERSHEY'S Semi-Sweet Chocolate Chips and 1 tablespoon shortening (do not use butter, margarine, spread or oil) in small microwave-safe bowl. Microwave at MEDIUM (50%) 30 seconds; stir. If necessary, microwave an additional 10 seconds or just until chips are melted and mixture is smooth when stirred.

tube & bundt cakes

Chocolate Syrup Swirl Cake

MAKES 20 SERVINGS

1	cup (2 sticks) butter or margarine, softened
2	cups sugar
2	teaspoons vanilla extract
3	eggs
2¾	cups all-purpose flour
1¼	teaspoons baking soda, divided
½	teaspoon salt
1	cup buttermilk or sour milk*
1	cup HERSHEY'S Syrup
1	cup MOUNDS Sweetened Coconut Flakes (optional)

To sour milk: Use 1 tablespoon white vinegar plus milk to equal 1 cup.

1 Heat oven to 350°F. Grease and flour a 12-cup fluted tube pan or 10-inch tube pan.

2 Beat butter, sugar and vanilla in large bowl until fluffy. Add eggs; beat well. Stir together flour, 1 teaspoon baking soda and salt; add alternately with buttermilk to butter mixture, beating until well blended.

3 Measure 2 cups batter in small bowl; stir in syrup and remaining ¼ teaspoon baking soda. Add coconut, if desired, to remaining vanilla batter; pour into prepared pan. Pour chocolate batter over vanilla batter in pan; do not mix.

4 Bake 60 to 70 minutes or until wooden pick inserted in center comes out clean. Cool 15 minutes; remove from pan to wire rack. Cool completely; glaze or frost as desired.

Brickle Bundt Cake

- 1⅓ cups (8-ounce package) HEATH BITS 'O BRICKLE Toffee Bits, divided
- 1¼ cups granulated sugar, divided
- ¼ cup chopped walnuts
- 1 teaspoon ground cinnamon
- ½ cup (1 stick) butter, softened
- 2 eggs
- 1¼ teaspoons vanilla extract, divided
- 2 cups all-purpose flour
- 1½ teaspoons baking powder
- 1 teaspoon baking soda
- ¼ teaspoon salt
- 1 container (8 ounces) dairy sour cream
- ¼ cup (½ stick) butter, melted
- 1 cup powdered sugar
- 1 to 3 tablespoons milk, divided

1 Heat oven to 325°F. Grease and flour 12-cup fluted tube pan or 10-inch tube pan. Set aside ¼ cup toffee bits for topping. Combine remaining toffee bits, ¼ cup granulated sugar, walnuts and cinnamon; set aside.

2 Beat remaining 1 cup granulated sugar and ½ cup butter in large bowl until fluffy. Add eggs and 1 teaspoon vanilla; beat well. Stir together flour, baking powder, baking soda and salt; gradually add to butter mixture alternately with sour cream, beating until blended. Beat 3 minutes. Spoon ⅓ of the batter into prepared pan. Sprinkle with half of toffee mixture. Spoon half of remaining batter into pan. Top with remaining toffee mixture. Spoon remaining batter into pan. Pour melted butter over batter.

3 Bake 45 to 50 minutes or until wooden pick inserted near center comes out clean. Cool 10 minutes; remove from pan to wire rack. Cool completely.

4 Stir together powdered sugar, 1 tablespoon milk and remaining ¼ teaspoon vanilla. Stir in additional milk, 1 teaspoon at a time, until desired consistency; drizzle over cake. Sprinkle with reserved ¼ cup toffee bits.

Chocolate Glazed Citrus Poppy Seed Cake

MAKES 12 SERVINGS

- **1** package (about 18 ounces) lemon cake mix
- **⅓** cup poppy seed
- **⅓** cup milk
- **3** eggs
- **1** container (8 ounces) plain lowfat yogurt
- **1** teaspoon freshly grated lemon peel
- **CHOCOLATE CITRUS GLAZE** (recipe follows)

1 Heat oven to 350°F. Grease and flour 12-cup fluted tube pan or 10-inch tube pan.

2 Combine cake mix, poppy seed, milk, eggs, yogurt and lemon peel in large bowl; beat until well blended. Pour batter into prepared pan.

3 Bake 40 to 45 minutes or until wooden pick inserted in center comes out clean. Cool 20 minutes; remove from pan to wire rack. Cool completely.

4 Prepare CHOCOLATE CITRUS GLAZE; spoon over cake, allowing glaze to run down sides.

Chocolate Citrus Glaze

- **2** tablespoons butter or margarine
- **2** tablespoons HERSHEY'S Cocoa or HERSHEY'S SPECIAL DARK Cocoa
- **2** tablespoons water
- **1** tablespoon orange-flavored liqueur (optional)
- **½** teaspoon orange extract
- **1¼** to 1½ cups powdered sugar

Melt butter in small saucepan over medium heat; remove from heat. Stir in cocoa, water, liqueur, if desired, and orange extract. Whisk in 1¼ cups powdered sugar until smooth. If glaze is too thin, whisk in remaining ¼ cup powdered sugar. Use immediately.

Chocolate Lemon Marble Cake

MAKES 16 TO 18 SERVINGS

- 2½ cups all-purpose flour
- 1¾ cups plus ⅓ cup sugar, divided
- 2 teaspoons baking powder
- 1¼ teaspoons baking soda, divided
- ½ teaspoon salt
- ⅓ cup butter or margarine, softened
- ⅓ cup shortening
- 3 eggs
- 1⅔ cups buttermilk or sour milk*
- 2 teaspoons vanilla extract
- ⅓ cup HERSHEY'S Cocoa
- ¼ cup water
- 2 teaspoons freshly grated lemon peel
- ¼ teaspoon lemon juice
- COCOA GLAZE (recipe follows)

To sour milk: Use 1 tablespoon plus 2 teaspoons white vinegar plus milk to equal 1⅔ cups.

1 Heat oven to 375°F. Grease and flour 12-cup fluted tube pan.**

2 Stir together flour, 1¾ cups sugar, baking powder, 1 teaspoon baking soda and salt in large bowl. Add butter, shortening, eggs, buttermilk and vanilla; beat on medium speed of electric mixer 3 minutes.

3 Stir together cocoa, remaining ⅓ cup sugar, remaining ¼ teaspoon baking soda and water; blend into ⅔ cup vanilla batter. Blend lemon peel and lemon juice into remaining vanilla batter; drop spoonfuls of lemon batter into prepared pan. Drop spoonfuls of chocolate batter on top of lemon batter; swirl with knife or metal spatula for marbled effect.

4 Bake 35 to 40 minutes or until wooden pick inserted in center comes out clean. Cool 15 minutes; remove from pan to wire rack. Cool completely. Glaze with COCOA GLAZE.

Cocoa Glaze

- ¼ cup HERSHEY'S Cocoa
- 3 tablespoons light corn syrup
- 4 teaspoons water
- ½ teaspoon vanilla extract
- 1 cup powdered sugar

Combine cocoa, corn syrup and water in small saucepan; cook over medium heat, stirring constantly, until mixture thickens. Remove from heat; blend in vanilla and powdered sugar. Beat until smooth.

MAKES ABOUT 1½ CUPS GLAZE

**Cake may also be baked in two 9×5×3-inch loaf pans. Bake 40 to 45 minutes or until wooden pick inserted in center comes out clean.*

Classic HERSHEY Bar Cake

MAKES 12 TO 16 SERVINGS

1	cup (2 sticks) butter or margarine, softened
1¼	cups granulated sugar
4	eggs
6	HERSHEY'S Milk Chocolate Bars (1.55 ounces each), melted
2½	cups all-purpose flour
¼	teaspoon baking soda
	Dash salt
1	cup buttermilk or sour milk*
½	cup HERSHEY'S Syrup
2	teaspoons vanilla extract
1	cup chopped pecans
	Powdered sugar (optional)

To sour milk: Use 1 tablespoon white vinegar plus milk to equal 1 cup.

1 Heat oven to 350°F. Grease and flour 10-inch tube pan or 12-cup fluted tube pan.

2 Beat butter in large bowl until creamy; gradually add granulated sugar, beating on medium speed of mixer until well blended. Add eggs, one at a time, beating well after each addition. Add chocolate; beat until blended.

3 Stir together flour, baking soda and salt; add to chocolate mixture alternately with buttermilk, beating until blended. Add syrup and vanilla; beat until blended. Stir in pecans. Pour batter into prepared pan.

4 Bake 1 hour and 15 minutes or until wooden pick inserted in center of cake comes out clean. Cool 10 minutes; remove from pan to wire rack. Cool completely. Sift powdered sugar over top, if desired.

Chocolate Quicky Sticky Bread

MAKES 12 SERVINGS

- **2** loaves (16 ounces each) frozen bread dough
- **¾** cup granulated sugar
- **1** tablespoon HERSHEY'S Cocoa
- **1** teaspoon ground cinnamon
- **½** cup (1 stick) butter or margarine, melted and divided
- **½** cup packed light brown sugar
- **¼** cup water
  HERSHEY'S MINI KISSESBRAND Milk Chocolates

1 Thaw loaves as directed on package; let rise until doubled.

2 Stir together granulated sugar, cocoa and cinnamon. Stir together ¼ cup butter, brown sugar and water in small microwave-safe bowl. Microwave at MEDIUM (50%) 30 to 60 seconds or until smooth when stirred. Pour mixture into 12-cup fluted tube pan.

3 Heat oven to 350°F. Pinch off pieces of bread dough; form into balls (1 ½ inches in diameter) placing 3 chocolate pieces inside each ball. Dip each ball in remaining ¼ cup butter; roll in cocoa-sugar mixture. Place balls in prepared pan.

4 Bake 45 to 50 minutes or until golden brown. Cool 20 minutes in pan; invert onto serving plate. Cool until lukewarm.

impressive cheesecakes

Toffee Bits Cheesecake

MAKES 10 TO 12 SERVINGS

CHOCOLATE CRUMB CRUST (recipe follows)

3	packages (8 ounces each) cream cheese, softened
¾	cup sugar
3	eggs
1⅓	cups (8-ounce package) HEATH BITS 'O BRICKLE Toffee Bits, divided
1	teaspoon vanilla extract
	Sweetened whipped cream

1 Prepare CHOCOLATE CRUMB CRUST. Heat oven to 350°F.

2 Beat cream cheese and sugar in large bowl until smooth. Add eggs, one at a time, beating well after each addition. Set aside 1 tablespoon toffee bits. Gently stir remaining toffee bits and vanilla into batter; pour into prepared crust.

3 Bake 45 to 50 minutes or until almost set. Remove from oven to wire rack. With knife, loosen cake from side of pan. Cool completely; remove side of pan.

4 Cover; refrigerate. Just before serving, garnish with whipped cream and reserved toffee bits. Cover; refrigerate leftover cheesecake.

Chocolate Crumb Crust: Heat oven to 350°F. Combine 1¼ cups vanilla wafer crumbs (about 40 wafers, crushed), ⅓ cup powdered sugar and ⅓ cup HERSHEY'S Cocoa in bowl; stir in ¼ cup (½ stick) melted butter or margarine. Press mixture firmly onto bottom and ½ inch up side of 9-inch springform pan. Bake 8 minutes; cool slightly.

HERSHEY'S SPECIAL DARK
Chocolate Layered Cheesecake

MAKES 10 TO 12 SERVINGS

CHOCOLATE CRUMB CRUST (recipe follows)

3 packages (8 ounces each) cream cheese, softened

¾ cup sugar

4 eggs

¼ cup heavy cream

2 teaspoons vanilla extract

¼ teaspoon salt

2 cups (12-ounce package) HERSHEY'S SPECIAL DARK Chocolate Chips, divided

½ teaspoon shortening (do not use butter, margarine, spread or oil)

1 Prepare CHOCOLATE CRUMB CRUST. Heat oven to 350°F.

2 Beat cream cheese and sugar in large bowl until smooth. Gradually beat in eggs, heavy cream, vanilla and salt, beating until well blended; set aside.

3 Set aside 2 tablespoons chocolate chips. Place remaining chips in large microwave-safe bowl. Microwave at MEDIUM (50%) 1½ minutes; stir. If necessary, microwave at MEDIUM an additional 15 seconds at a time, stirring after each heating, until chocolate is melted when stirred.

4 Gradually blend 1½ cups cheesecake batter into melted chocolate. Spread 2 cups chocolate mixture in prepared crust.

5 Blend another 2 cups plain cheesecake batter into remaining chocolate mixture; spread 2 cups of this mixture over first layer. Stir remaining cheesecake batter into remaining chocolate mixture; spread over second layer.

6 Bake 50 to 55 minutes or until center is almost set. Remove from oven to wire rack. With knife, immediately loosen cake from side of pan. Cool to room temperature.

7 Place reserved chocolate chips and shortening in small microwave-safe bowl. Microwave at MEDIUM 30 seconds; stir. If necessary, microwave at MEDIUM an additional 10 seconds at a time, stirring after each heating, until chocolate is melted and smooth when stirred. Drizzle over top of cheesecake. Cover; refrigerate several hours until cold. Cover and refrigerate leftover cheesecake.

Chocolate Crumb Crust: Stir together 1½ cups vanilla wafer crumbs (about 45 wafers, crushed), ½ cup powdered sugar and ¼ cup HERSHEY'S Cocoa; stir in ¼ cup (½ stick) melted butter or margarine. Press mixture onto bottom and 1½ inches up sides of 9-inch springform pan.

Brownie Sundae Cheesecake

MAKES 10 TO 12 SERVINGS

1 cup (¾-inch) brownie pieces (recipe follows)

   CHOCOLATE CRUMB CRUST (recipe follows)

4 packages (8 ounces each) cream cheese, softened

1 cup sugar

1½ teaspoons vanilla extract

4 eggs

¼ cup REESE'S Chocolate Peanut Butter Topping or ¼ cup HERSHEY'S Hot Fudge thinned with 1 teaspoon milk

1 Prepare brownie using recipe below or your own favorite recipe.

2 Heat oven to 350°F. Prepare CHOCOLATE CRUMB CRUST; cool slightly. Beat cream cheese, sugar and vanilla until smooth. Gradually add eggs, beating well after each addition. Pour batter into prepared crust.

3 Sprinkle brownie pieces over cheesecake surface; push pieces into batter. Drop topping by teaspoonfuls onto surface of cheesecake. With knife or metal spatula, swirl gently through batter for marbled effect. Bake 50 to 55 minutes or until almost set.* Remove from oven to wire rack. With knife, loosen cake from side of pan; cool.

4 Cover; refrigerate. Just before serving, garnish as desired. Cover; refrigerate leftover cheesecake.

Cheesecakes are less likely to crack if baked in a waterbath.

Chocolate Crumb Crust: Heat oven to 350°F. Combine 1½ cups vanilla wafer crumbs (about 45 wafers, crushed), 6 tablespoons powdered sugar, 6 tablespoons HERSHEY'S Cocoa and 6 tablespoons butter or margarine, melted. Press crumb mixture onto bottom and ½ to 1 inch up side of 9-inch springform pan. Bake 8 minutes; cool slightly.

Best Brownies

½ cup (1 stick) butter or margarine, melted

1 cup sugar

1 teaspoon vanilla extract

2 eggs

½ cup all-purpose flour

⅓ cup HERSHEY'S Cocoa

¼ teaspoon baking powder

¼ teaspoon salt

Heat oven to 350°F. Grease 8- or 9-inch square baking pan. Stir together butter, sugar and vanilla in bowl. Add eggs; beat well with spoon. Stir together flour, cocoa, baking powder and salt; gradually add to egg mixture, beating until well blended. Spread batter in prepared pan. Bake 20 to 25 minutes or until brownies begin to pull away from sides of pan. Cool completely in pan on wire rack.

MAKES 10 TO 12 SERVINGS

Chocolate & Peanut Butter Fudge Cheesecake

MAKES 10 TO 12 SERVINGS

1½ cups vanilla wafer crumbs (about 45 wafers, crushed)

½ cup powdered sugar

¼ cup HERSHEY'S Cocoa

⅓ cup butter or margarine, melted

3 packages (8 ounces each) cream cheese, softened

¾ cup granulated sugar

3 eggs

⅓ cup dairy sour cream

3 tablespoons all-purpose flour

1 teaspoon vanilla extract

¼ teaspoon salt

1 cup HERSHEY'S SPECIAL DARK Chocolate Chips or HERSHEY'S Semi-Sweet Chocolate Chips, melted

1 cup REESE'S Peanut Butter Chips, melted

HERSHEY'S Fudge Topping (optional)

Sweetened whipped cream (optional)

1 Heat oven to 350°F. Combine vanilla wafer crumbs, powdered sugar, cocoa and melted butter in medium bowl. Press onto bottom and 1 inch up side of 9-inch springform pan. Bake 8 minutes; cool.

2 Beat cream cheese and granulated sugar in large bowl until smooth. Add eggs, sour cream, flour, vanilla and salt; beat until well blended.

3 Place half of batter in separate bowl. Stir melted chocolate into one bowl of cream cheese mixture and melted peanut butter chips into the other. Spread chocolate mixture in prepared crust. Gently spread peanut butter mixture over chocolate mixture. Do not stir.

4 Bake 50 to 55 minutes or until center is almost set.* Remove from oven to wire rack. With knife, loosen cake from side of pan. Cool completely; remove side of pan. Cover; refrigerate.

5 To serve, drizzle each slice with fudge topping and top with whipped cream, if desired. Cover; refrigerate leftover cheesecake.

Cheesecakes are less likely to crack if baked in a waterbath.

HERSHEY'S SPECIAL DARK
Truffle Brownie Cheesecake

MAKES 10 TO 12 SERVINGS

BROWNIE LAYER

6	tablespoons melted butter or margarine
1¼	cups sugar
1	teaspoon vanilla extract
2	eggs
1	cup plus 2 tablespoons all-purpose flour
⅓	cup HERSHEY'S Cocoa
½	teaspoon baking powder
½	teaspoon salt

TRUFFLE CHEESECAKE LAYER

3	packages (8 ounces each) cream cheese, softened
¾	cup sugar
4	eggs
¼	cup heavy cream
2	teaspoons vanilla extract
¼	teaspoon salt
2	cups (12-ounce package) HERSHEY'S SPECIAL DARK Chocolate Chips, divided
½	teaspoon shortening (do not use butter, margarine, spread or oil)

1 Heat oven to 350°F. Grease 9-inch springform pan.

2 For BROWNIE LAYER, stir together melted butter, 1¼ cups sugar and 1 teaspoon vanilla. Add 2 eggs; stir until blended. Stir in flour, cocoa, baking powder and ½ teaspoon salt; blend well. Spread in prepared pan. Bake 25 to 30 minutes or until brownie layer pulls away from sides of pan.

3 Meanwhile for TRUFFLE CHEESECAKE LAYER, beat cream cheese and ¾ cup sugar with electric mixer on medium speed in large bowl until smooth. Gradually beat in 4 eggs, heavy cream, 2 teaspoons vanilla and ¼ teaspoon salt until well blended.

4 Set aside 2 tablespoons chocolate chips. Place remaining chips in large microwave-safe bowl. Microwave at MEDIUM (50%) 1½ minutes or until chips are melted and smooth when stirred. Gradually blend melted chocolate into cheesecake batter.

5 Remove BROWNIE LAYER from oven and immediately spoon cheesecake mixture over brownie. Return to oven; continue baking 45 to 50 minutes or until center is almost set. Remove from oven to wire rack. With knife, loosen cake from side of pan. Cool to room temperature. Remove side of pan.

6 Place remaining 2 tablespoons chocolate chips and shortening in small microwave-safe bowl. Microwave at MEDIUM 30 seconds or until chips are melted and mixture is smooth when stirred. Drizzle over top of cheesecake. Cover; refrigerate several hours until cold. Garnish as desired. Cover and refrigerate leftover cheesecake.

Three Layer Cheesecake Squares

CHOCOLATE CRUMB CRUST (recipe follows)

3   packages (8 ounces each) cream cheese, softened

¾   cup sugar

3   eggs

⅓   cup dairy sour cream

3   tablespoons all-purpose flour

1   teaspoon vanilla extract

1   cup REESE'S Peanut Butter Chips, melted

1   cup HERSHEY'S SPECIAL DARK Chocolate Chips or HERSHEY'S Semi-Sweet Chocolate Chips, melted

1   cup HERSHEY'S Premier White Chips, melted

THREE LAYER DRIZZLE (recipe follows)

1 Heat oven to 350°F. Line 9-inch square baking pan with foil, extending edges over pan sides; grease lightly. Prepare CHOCOLATE CRUMB CRUST.

2 Beat cream cheese and sugar until smooth. Gradually add eggs, sour cream, flour and vanilla; beat well. Stir 1⅓ cups batter into melted peanut butter chips; pour into prepared crust. Stir 1⅓ cups batter into melted chocolate chips; carefully spoon over peanut butter layer. Stir remaining batter into melted white chips; carefully spoon over chocolate layer.

3 Bake 40 to 45 minutes or until almost set. Cool completely on wire rack.

4 Prepare THREE LAYER DRIZZLE. Drizzle, one flavor at a time, over cheesecake. Refrigerate about 3 hours or until drizzle is firm. Use foil to lift cheesecake out of pan; cut into squares. Garnish as desired. Cover; refrigerate leftover cheesecake.

Chocolate Crumb Crust: Heat oven to 350°F. Combine 1½ cups vanilla wafer crumbs (about 45 wafers, crushed), 6 tablespoons powdered sugar, 6 tablespoons HERSHEY'S Cocoa and 6 tablespoons melted butter or margarine. Press onto bottom of prepared pan. Bake 8 minutes; cool slightly.

Three Layer Drizzle: Melt 1 tablespoon REESE'S Peanut Butter Chips with ½ teaspoon shortening, stirring until chips are melted and mixture is smooth. Repeat with 1 tablespoon HERSHEY'S SPECIAL DARK Chocolate Chips or HERSHEY'S Semi-Sweet Chocolate Chips with ½ teaspoon shortening and 1 tablespoon HERSHEY'S Premier White Chips with ½ teaspoon shortening.

Rich HEATH Bits Cheesecake

MAKES 12 TO 16 SERVINGS

VANILLA WAFER CRUST (recipe follows)

3 **packages (8 ounces each) cream cheese, softened**

1 **cup sugar**

3 **eggs**

1 **container (8 ounces) dairy sour cream**

½ **teaspoon vanilla extract**

1⅓ **cups (8-ounce package) HEATH Milk Chocolate Toffee Bits, divided**

1 Prepare VANILLA WAFER CRUST. Heat oven to 350°F.

2 Beat cream cheese and sugar in large bowl on medium speed of mixer until well blended. Add eggs, one at a time, beating well after each addition. Add sour cream and vanilla; beat on low speed until blended.

3 Pour half of cheese mixture into crust. Reserve ¼ cup toffee bits for topping; sprinkle remaining toffee bits over cheese mixture in pan. Spoon in remaining cheese mixture.

4 Bake 1 hour or until filling is set. Cool 15 minutes. Sprinkle reserved toffee bits over top; with knife, loosen cake from side of pan. Cool completely; remove side of pan. Cover, refrigerate at least 4 hours before serving. Cover; refrigerate leftover cheesecake.

Vanilla Wafer Crust: Combine 1¾ cups vanilla wafer crumbs (about 55 wafers, crushed) and 2 tablespoons sugar; stir in ¼ cup (½ stick) melted butter or margarine. Press onto bottom and 1 inch up side of 9-inch springform pan. Refrigerate about 30 minutes.

Chilled Raspberry Cheesecake

MAKES 10 TO 12 SERVINGS

- 1½ cups vanilla wafer crumbs (about 45 wafers, crushed)
- ⅓ cup HERSHEY'S Cocoa
- ⅓ cup powdered sugar
- ⅓ cup butter or margarine, melted
- 1 package (10 ounces) frozen raspberries (about 2½ cups), thawed
- 1 envelope unflavored gelatin
- ½ cup cold water
- ½ cup boiling water
- 2 packages (8 ounces each) cream cheese, softened
- ½ cup granulated sugar
- 1 teaspoon vanilla extract
- 3 tablespoons seedless red raspberry preserves
- CHOCOLATE WHIPPED CREAM (recipe follows)

1 Heat oven to 350°F.

2 Stir together vanilla wafer crumbs, ⅓ cup cocoa and ⅓ cup powdered sugar in medium bowl; stir in melted butter. Press mixture onto bottom and 1½ inches up side of 9-inch springform pan. Bake 10 minutes; cool completely.

3 Purée and strain raspberries; set aside. Sprinkle gelatin over cold water in small bowl; let stand several minutes to soften. Add boiling water; stir until gelatin dissolves completely and mixture is clear. Beat cream cheese, granulated sugar and 1 teaspoon vanilla in large bowl until smooth. Gradually add raspberry purée and gelatin, mixing thoroughly; pour into prepared crust.

4 Refrigerate several hours or overnight. Loosen cake from side of pan with knife; remove side of pan. Stir raspberry preserves to soften; spread over cheesecake top. Garnish with CHOCOLATE WHIPPED CREAM. Cover; refrigerate leftovers.

Chocolate Whipped Cream: Stir together ½ cup powdered sugar and ¼ cup HERSHEY'S Cocoa in medium bowl. Add 1 cup (½ pint) cold whipping cream and 1 teaspoon vanilla extract; beat until stiff.

Fudgey Chocolate Cheesecake with Butter Pecan Sauce

MAKES 12 SERVINGS

PECAN-CRUMB CRUST (recipe follows)

3   packages (8 ounces each) cream cheese, softened

1¼ cups sugar

2   teaspoons vanilla extract

3   eggs

½   cup HERSHEY'S Cocoa

BUTTER PECAN SAUCE (recipe follows)

Sweetened whipped cream (optional)

1 Prepare PECAN-CRUMB CRUST. Heat oven to 350°F.

2 Beat cream cheese in large bowl until fluffy. Add sugar and vanilla; beat on medium speed of mixer until well blended. Add eggs; beat well. Add cocoa; beat just until blended. Pour mixture over crust.

3 Bake 35 to 40 minutes or until set. (Center will be moist.) Remove from oven to wire rack. With knife, loosen cake from side of pan. Cool completely. Remove side of pan. Refrigerate until cold.

4 Serve with BUTTER PECAN SAUCE. Garnish with whipped cream, if desired. Cover; refrigerate leftover cheesecake.

Pecan-Crumb Crust: Heat oven to 350°F. Stir together 1½ cups vanilla wafer crumbs (about 45 wafers, crushed), ⅓ cup finely chopped pecans and ⅓ cup melted butter or margarine in medium bowl. Press mixture onto bottom of 9-inch springform pan. Bake 8 minutes. Cool slightly.

Butter Pecan Sauce

⅓   cup butter or margarine

1   cup packed light brown sugar

⅓   cup whipping cream

2   tablespoons light corn syrup

½   cup coarsely chopped pecans

1   teaspoon vanilla extract

Melt butter in small saucepan over medium heat. Add brown sugar, whipping cream and corn syrup. Cook, stirring constantly, until mixture boils. Remove from heat; stir in pecans and vanilla. Serve warm or cool.

MAKES ABOUT 1⅔ CUPS SAUCE

REESE'S Marble Cheesecake

CRUMB CRUST (recipe follows)

3   packages (8 ounces each) cream cheese, softened

1   cup sugar, divided

½   cup dairy sour cream

1   tablespoon vanilla extract

3   eggs

3   tablespoons all-purpose flour

¼   cup HERSHEY'S Cocoa

1   tablespoon vegetable oil

1⅓ cups REESE'S Peanut Butter Chips (reserved from crust)

¼   cup milk

1 Heat oven to 450°F. Prepare CRUMB CRUST.

2 Beat cream cheese, ¾ cup sugar, sour cream and vanilla in large bowl on medium speed of electric mixer until smooth. Add eggs and flour; beat until blended.

3 Beat cocoa, remaining ¼ cup sugar and oil with 1½ cups cheese mixture in medium bowl. Place 1⅓ cups peanut butter chips and milk in small microwave-safe bowl. Microwave at MEDIUM (50%) 30 seconds; stir. If necessary, microwave at MEDIUM an additional 15 seconds at a time, stirring after each heating, until chips are melted when stirred. Gradually add warm peanut butter mixture to remaining vanilla batter; beat on high speed 5 minutes.

4 Spoon peanut butter and chocolate mixtures alternately over prepared crust. Gently swirl with knife or spatula for marbled effect.

5 Bake 10 minutes.* Without opening oven door, decrease temperature to 250°F. and continue to bake 30 minutes. Turn off oven; leave cheesecake in oven 30 minutes without opening door. Remove from oven to wire rack; with knife, loosen cake from side of pan. Cool completely; remove side of pan. Refrigerate until serving time. Cover; refrigerate leftover cheesecake.

*Cheesecakes are less likely to crack if baked in a waterbath.

Crumb Crust

1⅔ cups (10-ounce package) REESE'S Peanut Butter Chips, divided

1¼ cups vanilla wafer crumbs (about 40 wafers, crushed)

¼   cup HERSHEY'S Cocoa

¼   cup powdered sugar

¼   cup (½ stick) butter or margarine, melted

With knife or food processor, chop ⅓ cup peanut butter chips (reserve remaining chips for cheesecake batter). Stir together crumbs, cocoa, powdered sugar and butter in medium bowl. Stir in chopped peanut butter chips. Press firmly onto bottom of 9-inch springform pan or 9-inch square pan.

Chocolate Cheesecake with Spiced Topping

MAKES 10 TO 12 SERVINGS

16   cinnamon grahams (2½-inch square each)

3   tablespoons butter or margarine, melted

2   packages (8 ounces each) cream cheese, softened

¾   cup sugar

⅓   cup HERSHEY'S Cocoa

2   eggs

1   teaspoon vanilla extract

SPICED TOPPING (recipe follows)

1 Heat oven to 350°F.

2 Crush cinnamon grahams to make 1 cup crumbs; mix crumbs and butter. Press mixture firmly onto bottom of 8-inch springform pan. Bake 8 minutes.

3 Increase oven temperature to 375°F. Beat cream cheese, sugar and cocoa in large bowl until creamy. Add eggs and vanilla, beating until blended; pour over crust. Bake 30 minutes. Carefully spread SPICED TOPPING over cheesecake. Continue baking 15 minutes or until topping is almost set. Loosen cake from side of pan. Cool; remove side of pan. Refrigerate at least 6 hours. Cover; refrigerate leftover cheesecake.

Spiced Topping

1   cup (8 ounces) sour cream

2   tablespoons sugar

½   teaspoon vanilla extract

¼   teaspoon ground cinnamon

Dash ground nutmeg

Stir together all ingredients in small bowl until well blended.

Ultra Chocolate Cheesecake

MAKES 12 SERVINGS

MOCHA CRUMB CRUST (recipe follows)

3 packages (8 ounces each) cream cheese, softened

1¼ cups sugar

1 container (8 ounces) dairy sour cream

2 teaspoons vanilla extract

½ cup HERSHEY'S Cocoa

2 tablespoons all-purpose flour

3 eggs

CHOCOLATE DRIZZLE (recipe follows)

1 Prepare MOCHA CRUMB CRUST. Heat oven to 350°F.

2 Beat cream cheese and sugar in large bowl until fluffy. Add sour cream and vanilla; beat until blended. Add cocoa and flour; beat until blended. Add eggs; beat well. Pour into crust.

3 Bake 50 to 55 minutes or until set. Remove from oven to wire rack. With knife, loosen cake from side of pan. Cool completely; remove side of pan. Prepare CHOCOLATE DRIZZLE; drizzle over top. Refrigerate 4 to 6 hours. Cover; refrigerate leftover cheesecake.

Chocolate Drizzle: Place ½ cup HERSHEY'S SPECIAL DARK Chocolate Chips or HERSHEY'S Semi-Sweet Chocolate Chips and 2 teaspoons shortening (do not use butter, margarine, spread or oil) in small microwave-safe bowl. Microwave at MEDIUM (50%) 30 seconds; stir. If necessary, microwave at MEDIUM an additional 10 seconds at a time, stirring after each heating, just until chips are melted and mixture is smooth.

Mocha Crumb Crust

1¼ cups vanilla wafer crumbs (about 40 wafers, crushed)

¼ cup sugar

¼ cup HERSHEY'S Cocoa

1 teaspoon powdered instant espresso or coffee

⅓ cup butter, melted

Heat oven to 350°F. Stir together crumbs, sugar, cocoa and instant espresso in medium bowl. Add butter; stir until well blended. Press mixture firmly onto bottom and 1 inch up side of 9-inch springform pan. Bake 8 minutes; cool slightly.

Creamy Ambrosia Cheesecake

MAKES 10 TO 12 SERVINGS

1 ⅓ cups graham cracker crumbs

½ cup MOUNDS Sweetened Coconut Flakes

¼ cup (½ stick) melted butter or margarine

1 ¼ cups plus 2 tablespoons sugar, divided

1 can (11 ounces) mandarin orange segments

1 can (8 ounces) crushed pineapple in juice

3 packages (8 ounces each) cream cheese, softened

3 eggs

2 cups (12-ounce package) HERSHEY'S Premier White Chips

TROPICAL FRUIT SAUCE (recipe follows)

Additional MOUNDS Sweetened Coconut Flakes

1 Heat oven to 350°F. Stir graham cracker crumbs, coconut, melted butter and 2 tablespoons sugar in medium bowl. Press mixture firmly onto bottom of 9-inch springform pan. Bake 8 minutes; cool slightly. Drain oranges and pineapple, reserving juices. Chop oranges into small pieces.

2 Beat cream cheese in large bowl until fluffy. Add remaining 1 ¼ cups sugar; beat well. Add eggs; beat well. Stir in white chips, oranges and pineapple. Pour mixture over crust.

3 Bake 60 to 65 minutes or until center is almost set. Remove from oven to wire rack. With knife, loosen cake from side of pan. Cool completely; remove side of pan. Cover; refrigerate until cold. Garnish with additional coconut, if desired, and serve with TROPICAL FRUIT SAUCE. Cover and refrigerate leftovers.

Tropical Fruit Sauce

Juice drained from 1 can (11-ounce-size) mandarin oranges

Juice drained from 1 can (8-ounce-size) crushed pineapple in juice

¼ cup sugar

1 tablespoon cornstarch

¼ teaspoon orange extract or pineapple extract

Combine fruit juices; pour 1 cup combined juice into medium saucepan and discard any remaining juices. Stir in sugar and cornstarch. Cook over medium heat, stirring constantly, until thickened. Remove from heat. Stir in orange extract or pineapple extract. Cool to room temperature before serving. Cover and refrigerate leftover sauce.

MAKES ABOUT ¾ CUP SAUCE

HERSHEY'S Double Chocolate Cheesecake

MAKES ABOUT 20 SQUARES OR 10 TO 12 WEDGES*

½	cup (1 stick) butter or margarine, softened
1¼	cups sugar, divided
¼	teaspoon salt
1	cup all-purpose flour
¼	cup HERSHEY'S Cocoa
2	packages (8 ounces each) cream cheese, softened
2	eggs
2	teaspoons vanilla extract
½	cup HERSHEY'S Mini Chips Semi-Sweet Chocolate
18	HERSHEY'S KISSESBRAND Milk Chocolates
	Sweetened whipped cream (optional)
	Additional HERSHEY'S KISSESBRAND Milk Chocolates (optional)

1 Heat oven to 350°F. Line 8- or 9-inch square baking pan* with foil, extending edges over pan sides.

2 Beat butter, ½ cup sugar and salt in small bowl until smooth. Stir together flour and cocoa; gradually add to butter mixture, beating on low speed of mixer until soft dough is formed. Press dough onto bottom of prepared pan.

3 Beat cream cheese and remaining ¾ cup sugar in medium bowl until smooth. Add eggs and vanilla; beat until well blended. Remove 1 cup batter; set aside. Add small chocolate chips to remaining batter; pour over crust.

4 Remove wrappers from 18 chocolates; place in medium microwave-safe bowl. Microwave at MEDIUM (50%) 1 minute; stir. If necessary, microwave at MEDIUM an additional 15 seconds at a time, stirring after each heating, until chocolate is melted and smooth when stirred. Add to reserved batter, stirring until well blended. Drop by spoonfuls onto batter in pan; gently swirl with knife or spatula for marbled effect.

5 Bake 35 to 40 minutes or until cheesecake is firm and top is slightly puffed. Cool completely in pan on wire rack. Cover; refrigerate several hours until chilled. To serve, lift from pan using foil edges; cut into squares. Garnish each square with whipped cream and chocolate pieces, if desired. Cover; refrigerate leftover cheesecake.

8- or 9-inch springform pan can also be used.

special occasion splurges

Chocolate Cherry Delight Cake

1	cup sugar
1	cup all-purpose flour
⅓	cup HERSHEY'S Cocoa
¾	teaspoon baking soda
¾	teaspoon baking powder
	Dash salt
½	cup milk
2	eggs
¼	cup vegetable oil
1	teaspoon vanilla extract
½	cup boiling water
1	container (8 ounces) frozen non-dairy whipped topping, thawed
1	can (21 ounces) cherry pie filling, chilled

1 Heat oven to 350°F. Line bottom of two 9-inch round pans with wax paper.

2 Combine sugar, flour, cocoa, baking soda, baking powder and salt in large bowl. Add milk, eggs, oil and vanilla; beat on medium speed of mixer 2 minutes. Stir in boiling water. (Batter will be thin.) Pour into prepared pans.

3 Bake 18 to 22 minutes or until wooden pick inserted in center comes out clean. Cool 10 minutes; remove from pans to wire racks. Carefully remove wax paper. Cool completely.

4 To assemble dessert, place one cake layer on serving plate. Spread with half of whipped topping; top with half of pie filling. Top with second cake layer. Spread with remaining topping and pie filling. Refrigerate at least 1 hour. Cover; refrigerate leftover cake.

Chocolate Almond Torte

- **4 eggs, separated**
- **¾ cup sugar, divided**
- **¾ cup ground blanched almonds**
- **⅓ cup all-purpose flour**
- **⅓ cup HERSHEY'S Cocoa**
- **½ teaspoon baking soda**
- **¼ teaspoon salt**
- **¼ cup water**
- **1 teaspoon vanilla extract**
- **¼ teaspoon almond extract**
- **CHERRY FILLING (recipe follows)**
- **CHOCOLATE GLAZE (recipe follows)**
- **Sliced almonds, maraschino cherries or candied cherries, halved**

1 Heat oven to 375°F. Grease bottoms of three 8-inch round baking pans. Line bottoms with wax paper; grease paper.

2 Beat egg yolks on medium speed of mixer 3 minutes in medium bowl. Gradually add ½ cup sugar; continue beating 2 minutes. Stir together almonds, flour, cocoa, baking soda and salt; add alternately with water to egg yolk mixture, beating on low speed just until blended. Stir in vanilla and almond extract.

3 Beat egg whites in large bowl until foamy; gradually add remaining ¼ cup sugar, beating until stiff peaks form. Fold small amount beaten egg whites into chocolate mixture; gently fold chocolate mixture into remaining whites just until blended. Spread batter evenly in prepared pans.

4 Bake 16 to 18 minutes or until top springs back when touched lightly in center. Cool 10 minutes; remove from pans to wire racks. Cool completely.

5 Prepare CHERRY FILLING. Place one cake layer on serving plate; spread half of filling over top. Repeat, ending with plain layer on top. Prepare CHOCOLATE GLAZE; spread on top of cake, allowing glaze to run down sides. Garnish with almonds and cherry halves. Refrigerate until glaze is set. Cover; refrigerate leftover torte.

Cherry Filling

- **1 cup (½ pint) cold whipping cream**
- **¼ cup powdered sugar**
- **1½ teaspoons kirsch (cherry brandy) or ¼ teaspoon almond extract**
- **⅓ cup chopped red candied cherries**

Beat whipping cream, powdered sugar and brandy until stiff; fold in cherries.

MAKES ABOUT 2 CUPS FILLING

Chocolate Glaze

1   **tablespoon butter or margarine**

2   **tablespoons HERSHEY'S Cocoa**

2   **tablespoons water**

1   **cup powdered sugar**

¼   **teaspoon vanilla extract**

Melt butter in small saucepan over low heat; add cocoa and water, stirring constantly until slightly thickened. Remove from heat; gradually add powdered sugar and vanilla, beating with whisk until smooth and of spreading consistency. Add additional water, ½ teaspoon at a time, if needed.

MAKES ABOUT ¾ CUP GLAZE

Jubilee Chocolate Cake

MAKES 12 TO 15 SERVINGS

¾   teaspoon baking soda

1   cup buttermilk or sour milk*

1½   cups cake flour or 1¼ cups all-purpose flour

1½   cups sugar, divided

½   cup HERSHEY'S Cocoa

½   teaspoon salt

½   cup vegetable oil

2   eggs, separated

½   teaspoon vanilla extract

Vanilla ice cream

FLAMING CHERRY SAUCE (recipe follows) or

QUICK AND EASY FLAMING CHERRY SAUCE (recipe follows)

To sour milk: Use 1 tablespoon white vinegar plus milk to equal 1 cup.

1 Stir baking soda into buttermilk in medium bowl until dissolved; set aside.

2 Heat oven to 350°F. Grease and flour 13×9×2-inch baking pan.

3 Stir together flour, 1 cup sugar, cocoa and salt. Add oil, buttermilk mixture, egg yolks and vanilla; beat until smooth. Beat egg whites in small bowl until soft peaks form; gradually add remaining ½ cup sugar, beating until stiff peaks form. Gently fold egg whites into chocolate batter. Pour batter into prepared pan.

4 Bake 30 to 35 minutes or until cake springs back when touched lightly in center. Cool in pan. Cut into squares; top each square with scoop of ice cream and serving of FLAMING CHERRY SAUCE.

Flaming Cherry Sauce

1   can (16 or 17 ounces) pitted dark or light sweet cherries, drained (reserve ¾ cup liquid)

1½   tablespoons sugar

1   tablespoon cornstarch

Dash salt

½   teaspoon freshly grated orange peel

¼   cup kirsch (cherry-flavored liqueur) or brandy

1 Stir together reserved cherry liquid, sugar, cornstarch and salt in chafing dish or medium saucepan. Cook over medium heat, stirring constantly, until mixture boils, about 1 minute. Add cherries and orange peel; heat thoroughly.

2 Gently heat liqueur in small saucepan over low heat; pour over cherry mixture. Carefully ignite with match. Stir gently; serve as directed. (Repeat procedure for sufficient amount of sauce for entire cake.)

MAKES 4 TO 6 SERVINGS

Quick and Easy Flaming Cherry Sauce: Combine 1 can (21 ounces) cherry pie filling with ¼ cup orange juice in chafing dish or medium saucepan; heat thoroughly. Gently heat ¼ cup kirsch (cherry-flavored liqueur) in small saucepan; pour over cherry mixture. Carefully ignite with match. Stir gently; serve as directed. (Repeat procedure for sufficient amount of sauce for entire cake.) Makes 6 to 8 servings.

Peanut Butter Holiday Cheesecake

- **6**   **tablespoons butter or margarine, melted**
- **6**   **tablespoons HERSHEY'S Cocoa**
- **⅓**   **cup powdered sugar**
- **1½**   **cups vanilla wafer cookie crumbs (about 45 cookies, crushed)**
- **1**   **package (8 ounces) cream cheese, softened**
- **2**   **tablespoons lemon juice**
- **1½**   **cups REESE'S Peanut Butter Chips**
- **1**   **can (14 ounces) sweetened condensed milk (not evaporated milk)**
- **1**   **cup (½ pint) whipping cream, whipped**
-     **CRANBERRY TOPPING (recipe follows)**

1 Stir together butter, cocoa, powdered sugar and vanilla wafer crumbs in bowl. Press firmly onto bottom of 9-inch springform pan; refrigerate while preparing filling.

2 Beat cream cheese and lemon juice in large bowl until fluffy; set aside. Combine peanut butter chips and sweetened condensed milk in medium saucepan over low heat; stir constantly until chips are melted and mixture is smooth. Add to cream cheese mixture; blend well. Fold in whipped cream. Pour evenly over crumb crust.

3 Cover; refrigerate while preparing CRANBERRY TOPPING. Spread topping evenly over cheesecake. Cover; refrigerate several hours or overnight. Remove side of springform pan to serve. Cover; refrigerate leftover cheesecake.

Cranberry Topping

- **2**   **cups fresh or frozen cranberries**
- **1**   **cup sugar**
- **¾**   **cup water, divided**
- **2**   **tablespoons cornstarch**
- **1**   **teaspoon vanilla extract**

1 Stir together cranberries, sugar and ½ cup water in medium saucepan. Cook over medium heat, stirring occasionally, until mixture comes to a boil. Reduce heat; simmer 3 minutes. Remove from heat.

2 Stir together cornstarch and remaining ¼ cup water; gradually add to cranberry mixture. Return to heat; stir constantly until mixture thickens and resembles fruit preserves (about 4 minutes). Cool to room temperature; stir in vanilla.

MAKES ABOUT 3½ CUPS TOPPING

German Black Forest Cherry Torte

- ⅔ cup unsalted butter
- 6 eggs
- 1 cup sugar
- 1 teaspoon vanilla extract
- ½ cup all-purpose flour
- ½ cup HERSHEY'S SPECIAL DARK Cocoa
- ¼ cup light corn syrup
- ¼ cup kirsch (cherry brandy)*
- 2 jars (10 ounces each) maraschino cherries, drained and rinsed
- WHIPPED CREAM FILLING AND TOPPING (recipe follows)

1 tablespoon almond extract plus 3 tablespoons water can be substituted for kirsch.

1 Heat oven to 350°F. Grease and flour three 8-inch round baking pans.

2 Melt butter over very low heat in small saucepan; remove from heat. Skim off milky solids and discard; reserve remaining butter. Beat eggs, sugar and vanilla on high speed in large bowl until mixture is thick, fluffy and very pale in color (about 10 minutes). Stir together flour and cocoa; sprinkle several tablespoons over top of egg mixture. Gently fold into egg mixture; repeat procedure until all of cocoa mixture is combined with egg mixture. Fold in melted butter, several tablespoons at a time. Divide mixture evenly among prepared pans.

3 Bake 10 to 15 minutes or until wooden pick inserted in center comes out clean. Cool 5 minutes; with knife, loosen cake from sides of pans. Invert onto wire racks; cool completely.

4 Place cake layers on wax paper; with fork, poke holes about 1-inch apart through all layers. Stir together corn syrup and kirsch; sprinkle evenly over cake layers. Lightly press cherries between layers of paper towels to remove excess moisture. Prepare WHIPPED CREAM FILLING AND TOPPING.

5 To assemble, place one layer on serving plate; spread with ½-inch layer of WHIPPED CREAM FILLING AND TOPPING. Place half of drained cherries over top, leaving 1 inch around edge free of cherries; with second layer, repeat procedure. Place third layer on top; frost and garnish top and sides with remaining WHIPPED CREAM FILLING AND TOPPING. Cover; refrigerate before serving. Garnish as desired.

Whipped Cream Filling and Topping:
Beat 3 cups (1½ pints) cold whipping cream, ½ cup powdered sugar and 1 teaspoon almond extract in large mixer bowl until stiff. Cover; refrigerate until ready to use.

Chocolate Rum Pecan Pound Cake

⅔ cup **HERSHEY'S Cocoa, divided**

¼ cup **boiling water**

1¼ cups **(2½ sticks) butter or margarine, softened**

2⅔ cups **sugar**

1 teaspoon **vanilla extract**

5 **eggs**

2 cups **all-purpose flour**

1 teaspoon **salt**

½ teaspoon **baking powder**

¼ teaspoon **baking soda**

½ cup **buttermilk or sour milk***

¾ cup **finely chopped pecans**

¼ cup **light rum or 1½ teaspoons rum extract plus ¼ cup water**

SATINY MINI CHIPS GLAZE (recipe follows)

To sour milk: Use 1½ teaspoons white vinegar plus milk to equal ½ cup.

1 Heat oven to 325°F. Grease and flour 12-cup fluted tube pan.

2 Stir ⅓ cup cocoa and water in small bowl until smooth; set aside. Beat butter, sugar and vanilla in large bowl until fluffy. Add eggs, one at a time, beating well after each addition. Add reserved cocoa mixture; beat well. Stir together flour, remaining ⅓ cup cocoa, salt, baking powder and baking soda; add to butter mixture alternately with buttermilk, beating well after each addition. Stir in pecans and rum. Pour batter into prepared pan.

3 Bake 1 hour and 5 minutes or until wooden pick inserted in center comes out clean. Cool 10 minutes; remove from pan to wire rack. Cool completely. Prepare SATINY MINI CHIPS GLAZE; drizzle over cake.

Satiny Mini Chips Glaze: Combine ¼ cup sugar and ¼ cup water in small saucepan. Cook over medium heat, stirring constantly, until sugar is dissolved and mixture begins to boil. Remove from heat; add 1 cup HERSHEY'S Mini Chips Semi-Sweet Chocolate, stirring until melted. Continue stirring until glaze is of desired consistency. Makes about 1 cup glaze.

Holiday Coconut Cake

MAKES 12 SERVINGS

- ½ cup (1 stick) butter or margarine, softened
- ½ cup shortening
- 2 cups sugar
- 5 eggs, separated
- 1 teaspoon vanilla extract
- 2 cups all-purpose flour
- 1 teaspoon baking soda
- ¼ teaspoon salt
- 1 cup buttermilk
- 2 cups MOUNDS Sweetened Coconut Flakes
- ½ cup chopped pecans
- **TOFFEE CREAM (recipe follows)**
- **Additional HEATH BITS 'O BRICKLE Toffee Bits (optional)**

1 Heat oven to 350°F. Grease and flour 12-cup fluted tube pan.

2 Beat butter, shortening, sugar, egg yolks and vanilla with electric mixer on medium speed in large bowl until creamy. Stir together flour, baking soda and salt; add alternately with buttermilk, beating until well blended. Stir in coconut and pecans.

3 Beat egg whites with electric mixer on high speed in large bowl until stiff peaks form; fold into batter. Pour batter into prepared pan.

4 Bake 45 to 55 minutes or until wooden pick inserted in center comes out clean. Cool 10 minutes; remove from pan to wire rack. Cool completely. Frost cake with TOFFEE CREAM. Garnish with additional toffee bits, if desired. Cover; store leftover cake in refrigerator.

Toffee Cream: Beat 2 cups (1 pint) whipping cream with ¼ cup powdered sugar and 1 teaspoon vanilla extract in large bowl until stiff peaks form. Fold in ½ cup HEATH BITS 'O BRICKLE Toffee Bits. Makes about 4 cups.

HERSHEY'S

Pies & Desserts

contents

PIES & DESSERTS

242

266

286

303

fruit pies & tarts

Fresh Apple and Toffee Tart

MAKES 2 TARTS (8 SERVINGS EACH)

4	to 6 large tart apples such as Granny Smith
¼	cup granulated sugar
2	tablespoons cornstarch or all-purpose flour
½	teaspoon ground cinnamon
1	package (15-ounce box) refrigerated pie crusts, softened as directed on box
1⅓	cups (8-ounce package) HEATH BITS 'O BRICKLE Toffee Bits, divided
2	teaspoons white decorator sugar crystals or granulated sugar, divided
	Sweetened whipped cream or ice cream (optional)

1 Heat oven to 400°F. Peel and slice apples into thin slices. Toss apples with granulated sugar, cornstarch and cinnamon.

2 Unroll crusts; place each on ungreased cookie sheet. Sprinkle ⅓ cup toffee bits over each crust; press lightly into crust.

3 Starting 2 inches from the edge of the crust, arrange apple slices by overlapping slightly in a circular spiral toward the center of the crust. Sprinkle ⅓ cup of remaining toffee bits over each apple center. Fold 2-inch edge of crust over apples. Sprinkle each crust edge with 1 teaspoon sugar crystals.

4 Bake 25 to 30 minutes or until crust is golden. Cool slightly. Serve warm or cool with sweetened whipped cream or ice cream, if desired.

Note: Recipe may be halved.

White Chip Fruit Tart

MAKES 10 TO 12 SERVINGS

¾ cup (1½ sticks) butter or margarine, softened

½ cup powdered sugar

1½ cups all-purpose flour

2 cups (12-ounce package) HERSHEY'S Premier White Chips

¼ cup whipping cream

1 package (8 ounces) cream cheese, softened

FRUIT TOPPING (recipe follows)

Assorted fresh fruit, sliced

1 Heat oven to 300°F.

2 Beat butter and powdered sugar in small bowl until smooth; blend in flour. Press mixture onto bottom and up side of 12-inch round pizza pan. Flute edge, if desired.

3 Bake 20 to 25 minutes or until lightly browned; cool completely.

4 Place white chips and whipping cream in medium microwave-safe bowl. Microwave at MEDIUM (50%) 1 to 1½ minutes or until chips are melted and mixture is smooth when stirred. Beat in cream cheese. Spread on cooled crust. Prepare FRUIT TOPPING. Arrange fruit over chip mixture; carefully pour or brush topping over fruit. Cover; refrigerate assembled tart until just before serving.

Fruit Topping

¼ cup sugar

1 tablespoon cornstarch

½ cup pineapple juice

½ teaspoon lemon juice

Stir together sugar and cornstarch in small saucepan; stir in juices. Cook over medium heat, stirring constantly, until thickened; cool.

Apple Toffee Crisp

MAKES 10 TO 12 SERVINGS

5	cups (about 5 medium apples) peeled and sliced Granny Smith apples
5	cups (about 5 medium apples) peeled and sliced McIntosh apples
1¼	cups sugar, divided
1¼	cups all-purpose flour, divided
¾	cup (1½ sticks) butter or margarine, divided
1⅓	cups (8-ounce package) HEATH BITS 'O BRICKLE Toffee Bits
1	cup uncooked rolled oats
½	teaspoon ground cinnamon
¼	teaspoon baking powder
¼	teaspoon baking soda
¼	teaspoon salt
	Whipped topping or ice cream (optional)

1 Heat oven to 375°F. Grease 13×9×2-inch baking pan.

2 Toss apple slices, ¾ cup sugar and ¼ cup flour, coating apples evenly. Spread in bottom of prepared pan. Dot with ¼ cup (½ stick) butter.

3 Stir together toffee bits, oats, remaining ½ cup sugar, remaining 1 cup flour, cinnamon, baking powder, baking soda and salt. Melt remaining ½ cup (1 stick) butter; add to oat mixture, mixing until crumbs are formed. Sprinkle crumb mixture over apples.

4 Bake 45 to 50 minutes or until topping is lightly browned and apples are tender. Serve warm with whipped topping or ice cream, if desired. Cover; refrigerate leftovers.

Secret Chocolate Strawberry Pie

MAKES 8 SERVINGS

3 cups sliced fresh strawberries (about 2½ pints), divided

1 cup sugar

2 teaspoons cornstarch

1 package (3 ounces) strawberry-flavored gelatin

1 tablespoon butter or margarine

1 tablespoon lemon juice

¼ cup HERSHEY'S SPECIAL DARK Chocolate Chips or HERSHEY'S Semi-Sweet Chocolate Chips

4 tablespoons whipping cream, divided

1 baked 9-inch pie crust, cooled

1 package (3 ounces) cream cheese, softened

Sweetened whipped cream (optional)

Whole strawberries (optional)

1 Reserve 2 cups sliced strawberries. Mash remaining 1 cup sliced strawberries; add enough water to make 2 cups. Stir together sugar and cornstarch in medium saucepan; stir in mashed strawberries. Cook over medium heat until mixture comes to a boil, stirring constantly; cook 2 minutes, stirring constantly. Remove from heat. Add gelatin, butter and lemon juice; stir until gelatin is dissolved. Strain mixture; discard seeds. Refrigerate until partially set.

2 Meanwhile, place chocolate chips and 3 tablespoons whipping cream in small microwave-safe bowl. Microwave at MEDIUM (50%) 1 minute; stir. If necessary, microwave at MEDIUM an additional 15 seconds at a time, stirring after each heating, just until chips are melted when stirred. Spread chocolate mixture onto bottom of prepared crust; refrigerate 30 minutes or until firm.

3 Beat cream cheese and remaining 1 tablespoon whipping cream in small bowl until smooth; spread over chocolate layer. Refrigerate filled crust while gelatin mixture is cooling.

4 When gelatin mixture is partially set, fold in reserved sliced strawberries; spoon mixture over cream cheese layer. Cover; refrigerate several hours or until firm. Just before serving, garnish with sweetened whipped cream and whole strawberries, if desired. Refrigerate leftover pie.

Chocolate Strawberry Fruit Tart

MAKES 12 SERVINGS

- 1⅓ cups all-purpose flour
- ½ cup powdered sugar
- ¼ cup HERSHEY'S Cocoa or HERSHEY'S SPECIAL DARK Cocoa
- ¾ cup (1½ sticks) butter or margarine, softened
- STRAWBERRY VANILLA FILLING (recipe follows)
- ½ cup HERSHEY'S SPECIAL DARK Chocolate Chips or HERSHEY'S Semi-Sweet Chocolate Chips
- 1 tablespoon shortening (do not use butter, margarine, spread or oil)
- GLAZED FRUIT TOPPING (recipe follows)
- Fresh fruit, sliced

1 Heat oven to 325°F. Grease and flour 12-inch pizza pan.

2 Stir together flour, powdered sugar and cocoa in medium bowl. With pastry blender, cut in butter until mixture holds together; press into prepared pan.

3 Bake 10 to 15 minutes or until crust is set. Cool completely.

4 Prepare STRAWBERRY VANILLA FILLING; spread over crust to within 1 inch of edge; refrigerate until filling is firm.

5 Place chocolate chips and shortening in small microwave-safe bowl. Microwave at MEDIUM (50%) 30 seconds; stir. If necessary, microwave at MEDIUM an additional 15 seconds at a time, stirring after each heating, just until chips are melted when stirred. Spoon chocolate into disposable pastry bag or corner of heavy duty plastic bag; cut off small piece at corner. Squeeze chocolate onto outer edge of filling in decorative design; refrigerate until chocolate is firm.

6 Prepare GLAZED FRUIT TOPPING. Arrange fresh fruit over filling; carefully brush prepared topping over fruit. Refrigerate until ready to serve. Cover; refrigerate leftover tart.

Strawberry Vanilla Filling

- 2 cups (12-ounce package) HERSHEY'S Premier White Chips
- ¼ cup evaporated milk
- 1 package (8 ounces) cream cheese, softened
- 1 teaspoon strawberry extract
- 2 drops red food color

1 Place white chips and evaporated milk in medium microwave-safe bowl. Microwave at MEDIUM (50%) 1 minute; stir. If necessary, microwave at MEDIUM an additional 15 seconds at a time, stirring after each heating, just until chips are melted when stirred.

2 Beat in cream cheese, strawberry extract and red food color.

Glazed Fruit Topping

¼ **teaspoon unflavored gelatin**

1 **teaspoon cold water**

1½ **teaspoons cornstarch or arrowroot**

¼ **cup apricot nectar or orange juice**

2 **tablespoons sugar**

½ **teaspoon lemon juice**

1 Sprinkle gelatin over water in small cup; let stand 2 minutes to soften.

2 Stir together cornstarch, apricot nectar, sugar and lemon juice in small saucepan. Cook over medium heat, stirring constantly, until mixture is thickened. Remove from heat; immediately stir in gelatin until smooth. Cool slightly.

nutty pies

Peanut Butter and Milk Chocolate Chip Cookie Pie

MAKES 8 TO 10 SERVINGS

½   cup (1 stick) butter or margarine, softened

2   eggs, beaten

2   teaspoons vanilla extract

1   cup sugar

½   cup all-purpose flour

1   cup HERSHEY'S Milk Chocolate Chips

1   cup REESE'S Peanut Butter Chips

1   cup chopped pecans or walnuts

1   unbaked (9-inch) pie crust

    Sweetened whipped cream or ice cream (optional)

1 Heat oven to 350°F.

2 Beat butter in medium bowl; add eggs and vanilla. Stir together sugar and flour; add to butter mixture. Stir in milk chocolate chips, peanut butter chips and nuts; pour into unbaked pie crust.

3 Bake 50 to 55 minutes or until golden brown. Cool about 1 hour on wire rack; serve warm with sweetened whipped cream or ice cream, if desired.

To Reheat: One slice at a time, microwave at HIGH (100%) 10 to 15 seconds.

Mocha Pecan Truffle Tart

- ½ cup (1 stick) butter or margarine, softened
- ¼ cup granulated sugar
- 3 eggs
- 1¼ cups all-purpose flour
- ½ cup ground toasted pecans*
- ¼ cup powdered instant coffee, divided
- 1 tablespoon water
- 1 can (14 ounces) sweetened condensed milk (not evaporated milk)
- 2 cups (12-ounce package) HERSHEY'S SPECIAL DARK Chocolate Chips or HERSHEY'S Semi-Sweet Chocolate Chips, divided
- 1 teaspoon vanilla extract
- ⅛ teaspoon salt
- ¾ cup coarsely chopped pecan pieces
- 1 cup (½ pint) heavy whipping cream, divided
- 2 tablespoons powdered sugar

To toast pecans: Heat oven to 350°F. Spread pecans in thin layer in shallow baking pan. Bake, stirring occasionally, 7 to 8 minutes or until golden brown; cool.

1 Heat oven to 350°F.

2 Beat butter and granulated sugar in medium bowl until fluffy; beat in 1 egg. Stir together flour and ground pecans; gradually beat into butter mixture, beating until well blended. Press mixture onto bottom and up side of 11-inch round tart pan with removable bottom. Place tart pan on baking sheet for additional support; bake 15 minutes.

3 Meanwhile, dissolve 3 tablespoons instant coffee in water in medium saucepan. Gradually stir in sweetened condensed milk; add 1 cup chocolate chips. Heat over low heat, stirring constantly, until chips are melted and mixture is well blended. Beat in remaining 2 eggs, vanilla and salt, blending well. Spread in partially baked crust.

4 Set aside 2 tablespoons chocolate chips; sprinkle remaining chips and chopped pecans over tart surface.

5 Bake 25 to 30 minutes or until filling is set and small cracks start to appear along the outer edge. Cool completely in pan on wire rack.

6 Place reserved 2 tablespoons chocolate chips and 1 tablespoon whipping cream in small microwave-safe bowl. Microwave at MEDIUM (50%) 15 to 20 seconds; stir until chips are melted and mixture is smooth. Drizzle over tart.

7 Combine remaining whipping cream, powdered sugar and remaining 1 tablespoon instant coffee in small mixer bowl. Beat until soft peaks form. Remove side of tart pan; cut into slices. Serve with whipped coffee cream and garnish as desired.

Butterscotch Nut Cookie Tart

MAKES 12 TO 16 SERVINGS

1   refrigerated pie crust (½ of 15-ounce package)

½   cup (1 stick) butter or margarine, softened

2   eggs, beaten

2   teaspoons rum extract

1   cup sugar

½   cup all-purpose flour

½   teaspoon salt

1   cup chopped walnuts

¾   cup plus 2 tablespoons (½ of 11-ounce package) HERSHEY'S Butterscotch Chips

Vanilla ice cream (optional)

1 Heat oven to 350°F. Unroll pastry; place in bottom and up sides of 9-inch springform pan.

2 Beat butter in medium bowl; add eggs and rum extract, blending well. Stir together sugar, flour and salt; beat into butter mixture. Stir in walnuts and butterscotch chips; spread in bottom of crust. Fold edges of crust loosely over filling, if desired.

3 Bake 45 to 50 minutes or until golden brown. Cool 10 minutes on wire rack; remove side of springform pan. Cool an additional hour. Best if served slightly warm. Cut into wedges and serve with vanilla ice cream, if desired.

Chocolate Pecan Pie

MAKES 8 SERVINGS

- **1** cup sugar
- **⅓** cup **HERSHEY'S** Cocoa
- **3** eggs, lightly beaten
- **¾** cup light corn syrup
- **1** tablespoon butter or margarine, melted
- **1** teaspoon vanilla extract
- **1** cup pecan halves
- **1** unbaked (9-inch) pie crust
- Whipped topping (optional)

1 Heat oven to 350°F.

2 Stir together sugar and cocoa in medium bowl. Add eggs, corn syrup, butter and vanilla; stir until well blended. Stir in pecans. Pour into unbaked pie crust.

3 Bake 60 minutes or until set. Remove to wire rack and cool completely. Garnish with whipped topping, if desired.

Fudgey Pecan Pie

MAKES 8 SERVINGS

⅓ cup butter or margarine

⅔ cup sugar

½ cup HERSHEY'S Cocoa

3 eggs

1 cup light corn syrup

¼ teaspoon salt

1 cup chopped pecans

1 unbaked (9-inch) pie crust

SWEETENED WHIPPED CREAM (recipe follows, optional)

Pecan halves (optional)

1 Heat oven to 375°F.

2 Melt butter in medium saucepan over low heat. Add sugar and cocoa; stir until well blended. Remove from heat; cool.

3 Beat eggs slightly in medium bowl. Stir in corn syrup and salt. Add cocoa mixture; blend well. Stir in chopped pecans. Pour into unbaked crust.

4 Bake 45 to 50 minutes or until set. Cool. For a crispy top on pie, cool and serve. For a softer pie on top, cool and cover; let stand about 8 hours before serving. Prepare and garnish pie with SWEETENED WHIPPED CREAM and pecan halves, if desired.

Fudgey Mocha Pecan Pie: Dissolve 1 teaspoon powdered instant coffee in 1 teaspoon hot water in small bowl or cup; add to pie filling when adding corn syrup and salt.

Sweetened Whipped Cream

½ cup cold whipping cream

1 tablespoon powdered sugar

¼ teaspoon vanilla extract

Stir together whipping cream, powdered sugar and vanilla in small bowl; beat on high speed of mixer until stiff.

MAKES ABOUT 1 CUP

Dark Fudgey Pecan Pie

MAKES 8 SERVINGS

1	unbaked (9-inch) pie crust
1½	cups coarsely chopped pecans
½	cup (1 stick) butter or margarine
1	cup light corn syrup
1	cup sugar
½	cup **HERSHEY'S SPECIAL DARK** Cocoa
4	eggs
1	teaspoon vanilla extract

1 Heat oven to 325°F. Fit pie crust into 9-inch pie plate according to package directions; fold edges under and crimp. Spread pecans evenly on bottom of pastry shell.

2 Combine butter, corn syrup, sugar and cocoa in medium saucepan; cook over low heat, stirring constantly, until sugar dissolves. Cool slightly. Stir in eggs and vanilla until blended. Pour into crust.

3 Bake 1 hour and 10 minutes or until set. Cool. Serve with whipped cream, if desired.

Note: To prevent overbrowning, cover edge of pie with foil.

Chocolate Harvest Nut Pie

MAKES 8 SERVINGS

- ½ cup packed light brown sugar
- ⅓ cup HERSHEY'S Cocoa
- ¼ teaspoon salt
- 1 cup light corn syrup
- 3 eggs
- 3 tablespoons butter or margarine, melted
- 1½ teaspoons vanilla extract
- ½ cup coarsely chopped pecans
- ½ cup coarsely chopped walnuts
- ¼ cup slivered almonds
- 1 unbaked (9-inch) pie crust
- Whipped topping (optional)

1 Heat oven to 350°F. Stir together brown sugar, cocoa and salt. Add corn syrup, eggs, butter and vanilla; stir until well blended. Stir in pecans, walnuts and almonds. Pour into unbaked pie crust. To prevent overbrowning of crust, cover edge of pie with foil.

2 Bake 30 minutes. Remove foil. Bake additional 25 to 30 minutes or until puffed across top. Remove from oven to wire rack. Cool completely.

3 Garnish with whipped topping and additional nuts, if desired. Cover; store leftover pie in refrigerator.

Fudge Brownie Pie

MAKES 6 TO 8 SERVINGS

2   **eggs**

1   **cup sugar**

½   **cup (1 stick) butter or margarine, melted**

½   **cup all-purpose flour**

⅓   **cup HERSHEY'S Cocoa**

¼   **teaspoon salt**

1   **teaspoon vanilla extract**

½   **cup chopped nuts (optional)**

    Ice cream

    HOT FUDGE SAUCE (recipe follows)

1 Heat oven to 350°F. Lightly grease 8-inch pie plate.

2 Beat eggs in medium bowl; blend in sugar and melted butter. Stir together flour, cocoa and salt; add to butter mixture. Stir in vanilla and nuts, if desired. Pour into prepared pie plate.

3 Bake 25 to 30 minutes or until almost set. (Pie will not test done in center.) Cool; cut into wedges. Serve topped with scoop of ice cream and drizzled with HOT FUDGE SAUCE.

Hot Fudge Sauce

¾   **cup sugar**

½   **cup HERSHEY'S Cocoa**

½   **cup plus 2 tablespoons (5-ounce can) evaporated milk**

⅓   **cup light corn syrup**

⅓   **cup butter or margarine**

1   **teaspoon vanilla extract**

1 Combine sugar and cocoa in small saucepan; blend in evaporated milk and corn syrup. Cook over medium heat, stirring constantly, until mixture boils; boil and stir 1 minute.

2 Remove from heat; stir in butter and vanilla. Serve warm sauce over ice cream or other desserts.

MAKES ABOUT 1¾ CUPS SAUCE

Microwave Directions: Stir together sugar and cocoa in medium microwave-safe bowl. Gradually add evaporated milk, stirring until blended. Stir in corn syrup. Microwave at HIGH (100%) 1 to 3 minutes, stirring after each minute, until mixture boils. Stir in butter and vanilla. Serve warm.

Mint Fudge Sauce: Add ¼ teaspoon mint extract with the vanilla.

Fudgey Mocha Nut Pie

MAKES 8 SERVINGS

- **6** tablespoons butter or margarine
- **⅓** cup HERSHEY'S Cocoa
- **1** can (**14 ounces**) sweetened condensed milk (not evaporated milk)
- **⅓** cup water
- **2** eggs, beaten
- **2** to 3 tablespoons powdered instant coffee
- **1** cup HERSHEY'S **SPECIAL DARK** Chocolate Chips or HERSHEY'S Semi-Sweet Chocolate Chips
- **1** cup coarsely chopped pecans
- **1** teaspoon vanilla extract
- **1** unbaked (**9-inch**) pie crust
- Sweetened whipped cream (optional)

1 Heat oven to 350°F.

2 Melt butter in medium saucepan over low heat. Add cocoa; stir until smooth. Stir in sweetened condensed milk, water, eggs, instant coffee and chocolate chips; whisk constantly until well blended and chocolate is melted. Remove from heat.

3 Stir in pecans and vanilla. Pour into unbaked pie crust.

4 Bake 40 minutes or until center is set. (Center will still appear moist.) Cool completely. Garnish with sweetened whipped cream, if desired. Cover; refrigerate leftover pie.

Chips and Bits Cookie Pie

MAKES 8 SERVINGS

½   cup (1 stick) butter or margarine, softened

2   eggs, beaten

2   teaspoons vanilla extract

1   cup sugar

½   cup all-purpose flour

1   cup HERSHEY'S SPECIAL DARK Chocolate Chips or HERSHEY'S Semi-Sweet Chocolate Chips

½   cup HEATH BITS 'O BRICKLE Toffee Bits

½   cup chopped pecans or walnuts

1   unbaked (9-inch) pie crust

    Ice cream or whipped cream (optional)

1 Heat oven to 350°F.

2 Beat butter with electric mixer on medium speed in large bowl until fluffy. Add eggs and vanilla; beat thoroughly. Stir together sugar and flour; add to butter mixture, mixing until well blended. Stir in chocolate chips, toffee bits and nuts; spread in unbaked pie crust.

3 Bake 45 to 50 minutes or until golden. Cool about 1 hour before serving; serve warm, or reheat cooled pie slices by microwaving on HIGH (100%) for about 10 seconds. Serve with ice cream or whipped cream, if desired.

cream pies

Classic Chocolate Cream Pie

MAKES 8 TO 10 SERVINGS

5   sections (½ ounce each) HERSHEY'S Unsweetened Chocolate Baking Bar, broken into pieces

3   cups milk, divided

1⅓ cups sugar

3   tablespoons all-purpose flour

3   tablespoons cornstarch

½   teaspoon salt

3   egg yolks

2   tablespoons butter or margarine

1½ teaspoons vanilla extract

1   baked (9-inch) pie crust, cooled, or 1 (9-inch) crumb crust

    Sweetened whipped cream (optional)

1 Combine chocolate and 2 cups milk in medium saucepan; cook over medium heat, stirring constantly, just until mixture boils. Remove from heat and set aside.

2 Stir together sugar, flour, cornstarch and salt in medium bowl. Whisk remaining 1 cup milk into egg yolks in separate bowl; stir into sugar mixture. Gradually add to chocolate mixture. Cook over medium heat, whisking constantly, until mixture boils; boil and stir 1 minute. Remove from heat; stir in butter and vanilla.

3 Pour into prepared crust; press plastic wrap directly onto surface. Cool; refrigerate until well chilled. Top with whipped cream, if desired.

Classic Boston Cream Pie

MAKES 8 TO 10 SERVINGS

⅓ cup shortening

1 cup sugar

2 eggs

1 teaspoon vanilla extract

1¼ cups all-purpose flour

1½ teaspoons baking powder

¼ teaspoon salt

¾ cup milk

RICH FILLING (recipe follows)

DARK COCOA GLAZE (recipe follows)

1 Heat oven to 350°F. Grease and flour 9-inch round baking pan.

2 Beat shortening, sugar, eggs and vanilla in large bowl until fluffy. Stir together flour, baking powder and salt; add alternately with milk to shortening mixture, beating well after each addition. Pour batter into prepared pan.

3 Bake 30 to 35 minutes or until wooden pick inserted in center comes out clean. Cool 10 minutes; remove from pan to wire rack. Cool completely.

4 Prepare RICH FILLING. With long serrated knife, cut cake in half horizontally. Place one layer, cut side up, on serving plate; spread with prepared filling. Top with remaining layer, cut side down. Prepare DARK COCOA GLAZE; spread over cake, allowing glaze to run down sides. Refrigerate several hours or until cold. Garnish as desired. Refrigerate leftover pie.

Rich Filling

⅓ cup sugar

2 tablespoons cornstarch

1½ cups milk

2 egg yolks, slightly beaten

1 tablespoon butter or margarine

1 teaspoon vanilla extract

Stir together sugar and cornstarch in medium saucepan; gradually add milk and egg yolks, stirring until blended. Cook over medium heat, stirring constantly, until mixture comes to a boil. Boil 1 minute, stirring constantly. Remove from heat; stir in butter and vanilla. Cover; refrigerate several hours or until cold.

MAKES ABOUT 1 ⅓ CUPS FILLING

Dark Cocoa Glaze

3 tablespoons water

2 tablespoons butter or margarine

3 tablespoons HERSHEY'S Cocoa

1 cup powdered sugar

½ teaspoon vanilla extract

Heat water and butter in small saucepan over medium heat until mixture comes to a boil; remove from heat. Immediately stir in cocoa. Gradually add powdered sugar and vanilla, beating with whisk until smooth and of desired consistency; cool slightly.

MAKES ABOUT ¾ CUP GLAZE

HERSHEY'S Cocoa Cream Pie

MAKES 6 TO 8 SERVINGS

1	baked (9-inch) pie crust or graham cracker crumb crust, cooled
1¼	cups sugar
½	cup **HERSHEY'S** Cocoa
⅓	cup cornstarch
¼	teaspoon salt
3	cups milk
3	tablespoons butter or margarine
1½	teaspoons vanilla extract
	Sweetened whipped cream

1 Prepare crust; cool.

2 Stir together sugar, cocoa, cornstarch and salt in medium saucepan. Gradually add milk, stirring until smooth. Cook over medium heat, stirring constantly, until mixture comes to a boil; boil 1 minute.

3 Remove from heat; stir in butter and vanilla. Pour into prepared crust. Press plastic wrap directly onto surface. Cool to room temperature. Refrigerate 6 to 8 hours. Serve with sweetened whipped cream. Garnish as desired. Cover; refrigerate leftover pie.

Easy Chocolate Coconut Cream Pie

- **1** unbaked (9-inch) pie crust
- **1** package (4-serving size) vanilla cook & serve pudding and pie filling mix*
- **½** cup sugar
- **¼** cup HERSHEY'S Cocoa or HERSHEY'S SPECIAL DARK Cocoa
- **1¾** cups milk
- **1** cup MOUNDS Sweetened Coconut Flakes
- **2** cups frozen whipped topping, thawed

Do not use instant pudding mix.

1 Bake pie crust; cool completely.

2 Stir together dry pudding mix, sugar and cocoa in large microwave-safe bowl. Gradually add milk, stirring with whisk until blended.

3 Microwave at HIGH (100%) 6 minutes, stirring with whisk every 2 minutes, until mixture boils and is thickened and smooth. If necessary, microwave an additional 1 minute; stir.

4 Cool 5 minutes in bowl; stir in coconut. Pour into prepared pie crust. Carefully press plastic wrap directly onto pie filling. Cool; refrigerate 6 hours or until firm. Top with whipped topping. Garnish as desired.

Creamy Milk Chocolate Pudding Pie

⅔ cup sugar

6 tablespoons cornstarch

2 tablespoons HERSHEY'S Cocoa

½ teaspoon salt

3 cups milk

4 egg yolks

2 tablespoons butter or margarine, softened

1 tablespoon vanilla extract

5 HERSHEY'S Milk Chocolate bars (1.55 ounces each), broken into pieces

1 packaged chocolate crumb crust (6 ounces)

Sweetened whipped cream or whipped topping

Additional HERSHEY'S Milk Chocolate Bar (1.55 ounces), cut into sections along score lines (optional)

1 Stir together sugar, cornstarch, cocoa and salt in 2-quart saucepan. Combine milk and egg yolks in bowl or container with pouring spout. Gradually blend milk mixture into sugar mixture.

2 Cook over medium heat, stirring constantly, until mixture comes to a boil. Boil and stir 1 minute. Remove from heat; stir in butter and vanilla. Add chocolate bar pieces; stir until melted and mixture is well blended. Pour into crumb crust; press plastic wrap onto filling. Cool. Refrigerate several hours or until chilled and firm. Remove plastic wrap. Garnish with whipped cream and chocolate bar sections, if desired. Cover; refrigerate leftovers.

Chocolate Bavarian Pie

MAKES 8 SERVINGS

1	envelope unflavored gelatin
1¾	cups milk, divided
⅔	cup sugar
6	tablespoons HERSHEY'S Cocoa
1	tablespoon light corn syrup
2	tablespoons butter
¾	teaspoon vanilla extract
1	cup (½ pint) cold whipping cream
1	baked (9-inch) pie crust or crumb crust
	HERSHEY'S Syrup

1 Sprinkle gelatin over 1 cup milk in medium saucepan; let stand 2 minutes to soften.

2 Stir together sugar and cocoa; add to milk mixture. Add corn syrup. Cook, stirring constantly, until mixture boils. Remove from heat. Add butter; stir until melted. Stir in remaining ¾ cup milk and vanilla. Pour into large bowl. Cool; refrigerate until almost set.

3 Beat whipping cream in small bowl on high speed of mixer until stiff. Beat chocolate mixture on medium speed until smooth. On low speed, add whipped cream to chocolate mixture, beating just until blended. Pour into prepared crust; refrigerate* until set, at least 3 hours. Just before serving, drizzle each pie slice with chocolate syrup. Cover; refrigerate leftover pie.

*FROZEN CHOCOLATE BAVARIAN PIE: Freeze pie 4 to 6 hours or overnight. Remove from freezer 10 to 15 minutes before serving.

Easy Peanut Butter Chip Pie

MAKES 6 TO 8 SERVINGS

- 1 package (3 ounces) cream cheese, softened
- 1 teaspoon lemon juice
- 1⅔ cups (10-ounce package) REESE'S Peanut Butter Chips, divided
- ⅔ cup sweetened condensed milk (not evaporated milk)
- 1 cup (½ pint) cold whipping cream, divided
- 1 packaged chocolate or graham cracker crumb crust (6 ounces)
- 1 tablespoon powdered sugar
- 1 teaspoon vanilla extract

1 Beat cream cheese and lemon juice in medium bowl until fluffy, about 2 minutes; set aside.

2 Place 1 cup peanut butter chips and sweetened condensed milk in medium microwave-safe bowl. Microwave at MEDIUM (50%) 45 seconds; stir. If necessary, microwave an additional 15 seconds at a time, stirring after each heating, until chips are melted and mixture is smooth when stirred.

3 Add warm peanut butter mixture to cream cheese mixture. Beat on medium speed until blended, about 1 minute. Beat ½ cup whipping cream in small bowl until stiff; fold into peanut butter mixture. Pour into crust. Cover; refrigerate several hours or overnight until firm.

4 Just before serving, combine remaining ½ cup whipping cream, powdered sugar and vanilla in small bowl. Beat until stiff; spread over filling. Garnish with remaining peanut butter chips. Cover; refrigerate leftover pie.

Chocolate-Cranberry Cream Cheese Pie

MAKES ABOUT 8 SERVINGS

1 ¼	cups graham cracker crumbs
⅓	cup butter, melted
¼	cup sugar
½	cup whipping cream
1	cup HERSHEY'S SPECIAL DARK Chocolate Chips or HERSHEY'S Semi-Sweet Chocolate Chips
1	cup HERSHEY'S Premier White Chips
1	package (8 ounces) cream cheese, softened
2	tablespoons orange juice
2	teaspoons freshly grated orange or lemon peel
	CRANBERRY TOPPING (recipe follows)

1 Heat oven to 375°F. Mix together graham cracker crumbs, butter and sugar in medium bowl until combined. Press mixture firmly onto bottom and side of 9-inch pie plate. Bake 8 to 10 minutes or until lightly browned. Cool on wire rack.

2 Heat cream in small saucepan over medium heat just to a boil. Remove from heat; add chocolate chips. Whisk until chocolate is melted and mixture is smooth. Spread onto bottom of crust. Cover; refrigerate 1 ½ hours or until chocolate is slightly firm.

3 Place white chips in small microwave-safe bowl. Microwave at MEDIUM (50%) 1 minute; stir. If necessary, microwave at MEDIUM an additional 15 seconds at a time, stirring after each heating, just until chips are melted and mixture is smooth.

4 Beat cream cheese in large bowl until smooth. Add melted white chips, orange juice and orange peel, beating until smooth. Spread mixture evenly over chocolate layer. Refrigerate 2 hours or until firm.

5 Meanwhile, prepare CRANBERRY TOPPING. To serve, spoon topping over each serving of pie.

Cranberry Topping: Stir together 1 bag (12 ounces) fresh or frozen cranberries, 1 cup sugar and ½ cup water in medium saucepan. Bring to a boil over medium heat, stirring occasionally. Continue to cook, uncovered, stirring often, about 3 to 5 minutes or until berries have popped. Remove from heat and cool. Cover; refrigerate until ready to use.* Makes about 2 cups topping.

Chilled topping may become thick; stir vigorously to soften.

PIES & DESSERTS

All-Chocolate Boston Cream Pie

MAKES 8 SERVINGS

- 1 cup all-purpose flour
- 1 cup sugar
- ⅓ cup HERSHEY'S Cocoa
- ½ teaspoon baking soda
- 6 tablespoons butter or margarine, softened
- 1 cup milk
- 1 egg
- 1 teaspoon vanilla extract

CHOCOLATE FILLING (recipe follows)

SATINY CHOCOLATE GLAZE (recipe follows)

1 Heat oven to 350°F. Grease and flour one 9-inch round baking pan.

2 Stir together flour, sugar, cocoa and baking soda in large bowl. Add butter, milk, egg and vanilla. Beat on low speed of mixer until all ingredients are moistened. Beat on medium speed 2 minutes. Pour batter into prepared pan.

3 Bake 30 to 35 minutes or until wooden pick inserted in center comes out clean. Cool 10 minutes; remove from pan to wire rack. Cool completely. Prepare CHOCOLATE FILLING. Cut cake into two thin layers. Place one layer on serving plate; spread filling over layer. Top with remaining layer.

4 Prepare SATINY CHOCOLATE GLAZE. Pour onto top of cake, allowing some to drizzle down sides. Refrigerate until serving time. Cover; refrigerate leftover cake.

Chocolate Filling

- ½ cup sugar
- ¼ cup HERSHEY'S Cocoa
- 2 tablespoons cornstarch
- 1½ cups light cream
- 1 tablespoon butter or margarine
- 1 teaspoon vanilla extract

Stir together sugar, cocoa and cornstarch in medium saucepan; gradually stir in light cream. Cook over medium heat, stirring constantly, until mixture thickens and begins to boil. Boil 1 minute, stirring constantly; remove from heat. Stir in butter and vanilla. Press plastic wrap directly onto surface. Cool completely.

Satiny Chocolate Glaze

- 2 tablespoons water
- 1 tablespoon butter or margarine
- 1 tablespoon corn syrup
- 2 tablespoons HERSHEY'S Cocoa
- ¾ cup powdered sugar
- ½ teaspoon vanilla extract

Heat water, butter and corn syrup in small saucepan to boiling. Remove from heat; immediately stir in cocoa. With whisk, gradually beat in powdered sugar and vanilla until smooth; cool slightly.

tortes

Easy MINI KISSES Cookie Torte

1	**cup sugar**
½	**cup HERSHEY'S Cocoa**
½	**cup strong coffee**
⅓	**cup shortening**
¼	**teaspoon ground cinnamon**
1	**package (11 ounces) pie crust mix**
2½	**cups cold whipping cream**
1¾	**cups (10-ounce package) HERSHEY'S MINI KISSES**BRAND **Milk Chocolates, divided**

1 Place sugar, cocoa, coffee, shortening and cinnamon in large microwave-safe bowl. Microwave at HIGH (100%) 1 minute; stir. Continue microwaving, 30 seconds at a time, until mixture is smooth and creamy when stirred with wire whisk. Remove ¾ cup of mixture; set aside remaining mixture.

2 Stir together pie crust mix and reserved ¾ cup cocoa mixture, blending until smooth. Shape into ball; cut into 4 pieces. Shape into patties; wrap in plastic wrap. Freeze for 10 minutes or just until firm, but pliable.

3 Meanwhile, heat oven to 350°F. Line two cookie sheets with foil; mark two 8-inch diameter circles on each. Place 1 patty in center of each circle; press with fingers into marked circles. Bake 10 to 12 minutes or until almost set; cool completely on foil.

4 Gently peel foil away from cookies. In bowl with remaining cocoa mixture, pour whipping cream; beat until whipped cream consistency, about 3 minutes. Place 1 cookie on serving plate; place chocolates all around the outside edge of cookie. Place one-fourth of cream mixture in center; gently spread out to chocolates.

5 Repeat layering with remaining 3 cookies, cream mixture and chocolates, ending with cream mixture. Place remaining chocolates on top of torte and garnish as desired. Cover; refrigerate 4 hours until filling has softened cookies. Refrigerate leftover torte.

Tuxedo Torte

MAKES 10 TO 12 SERVINGS

½	cup (1 stick) butter or margarine, melted
1¼	cups granulated sugar
1	teaspoon vanilla extract
2	eggs
⅔	cup all-purpose flour
½	cup HERSHEY'S Cocoa
¼	teaspoon baking powder
¼	teaspoon salt
1	package (8 ounces) cream cheese, softened
1	cup powdered sugar
¾	cup heavy cream, divided
28	HERSHEY'S KISSESBRAND Milk Chocolates*

Whipped topping or sweetened whipped cream (optional)

Additional HERSHEY'S KISSESBRAND Milk Chocolates (optional)

HERSHEY'S HUGSBRAND Candies (optional)

*¾ cup HERSHEY'S MINI KISSESBRAND Milk Chocolates may be substituted for HERSHEY'S KISSESBRAND Milk Chocolates.

1 Heat oven to 350°F. Line 9-inch round cake pan with foil, extending foil beyond sides. Grease foil.

2 Stir together melted butter, granulated sugar and vanilla in large bowl. Add eggs; beat well using spoon. Stir together flour, cocoa, baking powder and salt; gradually add to egg mixture, beating with spoon until well blended. Spread batter in prepared pan.

3 Bake 25 minutes or until cake is set. (Cake will be fudgey and will not test done.) Remove from oven; cool completely in pan on wire rack.

4 Beat cream cheese and powdered sugar in medium bowl until well blended. Beat ½ cup heavy cream until stiff; gradually fold into cream cheese mixture, blending well. Spread over brownie layer. Cover; refrigerate at least 1 hour.

5 Remove wrappers from 28 milk chocolates; place in medium microwave-safe bowl with remaining ¼ cup heavy cream. Microwave at MEDIUM (50%) 1 minute; stir. If necessary, microwave at MEDIUM an additional 10 seconds at a time, stirring after each heating, until chocolates are melted and mixture is smooth when stirred. Cool slightly; pour and spread over cream cheese mixture.

6 Cover; refrigerate about 2 hours or until chilled. Use foil to lift out of pan; remove foil. Cut into wedges; serve garnished with whipped topping, chocolates and chocolate candies, if desired. Cover; refrigerate leftover dessert.

Cherry Glazed Chocolate Torte

MAKES 10 TO 12 SERVINGS

½   cup (1 stick) butter or margarine, melted

1   cup granulated sugar

1   teaspoon vanilla extract

2   eggs

½   cup all-purpose flour

⅓   cup HERSHEY'S Cocoa

¼   teaspoon baking powder

¼   teaspoon salt

1   package (8 ounces) cream cheese, softened

1   cup powdered sugar

1   cup frozen non-dairy whipped topping, thawed

1   can (21 ounces) cherry pie filling, divided

1 Heat oven to 350°F. Grease bottom of 9-inch springform pan.

2 Stir together butter, granulated sugar and vanilla in large bowl. Add eggs; using spoon, beat well. Stir together flour, cocoa, baking powder and salt; gradually add to egg mixture, beating until well blended. Spread batter in prepared pan.

3 Bake 25 to 30 minutes or until cake is set. (Cake will be fudgey and will not test done.) Remove from oven; cool completely in pan on wire rack.

4 Beat cream cheese and powdered sugar in medium bowl until well blended; gradually fold in whipped topping, blending well. Spread over top of cake. Spread 1 cup cherry pie filling over cream layer; refrigerate several hours. With knife, loosen cake from side of pan; remove side of pan. Cut into wedges; garnish with remaining pie filling. Cover; refrigerate leftover dessert.

HERSHEY'S White and Dark Chocolate Fudge Torte

MAKES 10 TO 12 SERVINGS

1   cup (2 sticks) butter or margarine, melted

1½ cups sugar

1   teaspoon vanilla extract

3   eggs, separated

⅔   cup HERSHEY'S Cocoa

½   cup all-purpose flour

3   tablespoons water

2   cups (12-ounce package) HERSHEY'S Premier White Chips, divided

⅛   teaspoon cream of tartar

    SATINY GLAZE (recipe follows)

    WHITE DECORATOR DRIZZLE (recipe follows)

1 Heat oven to 350°F. Line bottom of 9-inch springform pan with foil; grease foil and side of pan.

2 Combine butter, sugar and vanilla in large bowl; beat well. Add egg yolks, one at a time, beating well after each addition. Blend in cocoa, flour and water. Stir in 1⅔ cups white chips. Reserve remaining chips for drizzle. Beat egg whites with cream of tartar in small bowl until stiff peaks form; fold into chocolate mixture. Pour batter into prepared pan.

3 Bake 45 minutes or until top begins to crack slightly. (Cake will not test done in center.) Cool 1 hour. Cover; refrigerate until firm. Remove side of pan. Prepare SATINY GLAZE and WHITE DECORATOR DRIZZLE. Pour prepared glaze over torte; spread evenly over top and sides. Decorate top of torte with prepared drizzle* or wait to prepare drizzle and decorate individual slices before serving. Cover; refrigerate until serving time. Refrigerate leftover torte.

To decorate, drizzle with spoon or place in pastry bag with writing tip.

Satiny Glaze

1   cup HERSHEY'S SPECIAL DARK Chocolate Chips or HERSHEY'S Semi-Sweet Chocolate Chips

¼   cup whipping cream

Place chocolate chips and whipping cream in small microwave-safe bowl. Microwave at MEDIUM (50%) 1 minute; stir. If necessary, microwave at MEDIUM an additional 15 seconds at a time, stirring after each heating, just until chips are melted when stirred. Cool until lukewarm and slightly thickened.

MAKES ABOUT ¾ CUP GLAZE

White Decorator Drizzle

⅓ cup HERSHEY'S Premier White Chips (reserved from torte)

2 teaspoons shortening (do not use butter, margarine, spread or oil)

Place white chips and shortening in small microwave-safe bowl. Microwave at MEDIUM (50%) 20 to 30 seconds; stir. If necessary, microwave at MEDIUM an additional 10 seconds at a time, stirring after each heating, just until chips are melted when stirred.

Flourless Chocolate Torte

MAKES 10 SERVINGS

1 ¼   **cups (2½ sticks) butter**

¾   **cup HERSHEY'S Cocoa**

2   **cups sugar, divided**

6   **eggs, separated**

¼   **cup water**

1   **teaspoon vanilla extract**

1   **cup blanched sliced almonds, toasted and ground***

½   **cup plain dry bread crumbs**

  MOCHA CREAM (recipe follows)

*To toast almonds: Heat oven to 350°F. Place almonds in single layer in shallow baking pan. Bake 7 to 8 minutes, stirring occasionally, until light brown. Cool.

1 Heat oven to 350°F. Grease and flour 9-inch springform pan. Melt butter in saucepan over low heat. Add cocoa and 1½ cups sugar; stir until smooth. Cool to room temperature.

2 Beat egg yolks in large bowl until thick. Gradually beat in chocolate mixture; stir in water and vanilla. Combine ground almonds and bread crumbs; stir into chocolate mixture.

3 Beat egg whites until foamy; gradually add remaining ½ cup sugar, beating until soft peaks form. Fold about one-third of egg whites into chocolate. Fold chocolate into remaining egg whites. Pour into prepared pan.

4 Bake 50 to 60 minutes or until wooden pick inserted in center comes out clean. Cool 10 minutes. Loosen cake from side of pan; remove pan. Cool completely. Spread MOCHA CREAM over top. Sift with cocoa just before serving. Store covered in refrigerator.

Mocha Cream: Combine 1 cup (½ pint) cold whipping cream, 2 tablespoons powdered sugar, 1½ teaspoons powdered instant coffee dissolved in 1 teaspoon water and ½ teaspoon vanilla extract in medium bowl; beat until stiff. Makes about 2 cups.

Berry-Berry Brownie Torte

MAKES 8 TO 10 SERVINGS

½	cup all-purpose flour
¼	teaspoon baking soda
¼	teaspoon salt
1	cup HERSHEY'S SPECIAL DARK Chocolate Chips or HERSHEY'S Semi-Sweet Chocolate Chips
½	cup (1 stick) butter or margarine
1¼	cups sugar, divided
2	eggs
1	teaspoon vanilla extract
⅓	cup HERSHEY'S SPECIAL DARK Cocoa or HERSHEY'S Cocoa
½	cup whipping cream
¾	cup fresh blackberries, rinsed and patted dry
¾	cup fresh raspberries, rinsed and patted dry

1 Heat oven to 350°F. Line 9-inch round baking pan with wax paper, then grease. Stir together flour, baking soda and salt. Stir in chocolate chips.

2 Melt butter in medium saucepan over low heat. Remove from heat. Stir in 1 cup sugar, eggs and vanilla. Add cocoa, blending well. Stir in flour mixture. Spread mixture in prepared pan.

3 Bake 20 to 25 minutes or until wooden pick inserted into center comes out slightly sticky. Cool in pan on wire rack 15 minutes. Invert onto wire rack; remove wax paper. Turn right side up; cool completely.

4 Beat whipping cream and remaining ¼ cup sugar until sugar is dissolved and stiff peaks form. Spread over top of brownie. Top with berries. Refrigerate until serving time.

Mocha Brownie Nut Torte

MAKES 10 TO 12 SERVINGS

- 1 cup (2 sticks) butter
- 1 package (4 ounces) HERSHEY'S Unsweetened Chocolate Baking Bar, broken into pieces
- 4 eggs
- 1 teaspoon vanilla extract
- 2 cups granulated sugar
- 1 cup all-purpose flour
- 1 cup finely chopped pecans
- 1 package (8 ounces) cream cheese, softened
- 1 cup powdered sugar
- ½ cup chilled whipping cream
- 2 to 3 teaspoons powdered instant coffee
- CHOCOLATE GLAZE (recipe follows)

1 Heat oven to 350°F. Line bottom and sides of 9-inch round cake pan with foil, extending foil beyond sides. Grease foil.

2 Place butter and chocolate in medium microwave-safe bowl. Microwave at MEDIUM (50%) 1 minute; stir. If necessary, microwave an additional 15 seconds at a time, stirring after each heating, until chocolate is melted when stirred. Cool 5 minutes.

3 Beat eggs and vanilla in large bowl until foamy. Gradually beat in granulated sugar. Blend in chocolate mixture; fold in flour and pecans. Spread mixture in prepared pan. Bake 40 to 45 minutes or until wooden pick inserted in center comes out clean. Cool completely in pan on wire rack.

4 Use foil to lift brownie from pan; remove foil. Place brownie layer on serving plate. Beat cream cheese and powdered sugar in medium bowl until well blended. Beat whipping cream and instant coffee until stiff; gradually fold into cream cheese mixture, blending well. Spread over brownie layer. Cover; refrigerate until serving time.

5 Just before serving, prepare CHOCOLATE GLAZE. Drizzle generous tablespoon glaze over top and down sides of each serving.

Chocolate Glaze: Place 6 ounces (1½ 4-ounce packages) HERSHEY'S Semi-Sweet Chocolate Baking Bar and ½ cup whipping cream in small microwave-safe bowl. Microwave at MEDIUM (50%) 30 to 45 seconds or until chocolate is melted and mixture is smooth when stirred. Cool slightly. Makes 1 cup glaze.

Chocolate and Cherries Fudge Torte

MAKES 10 TO 12 SERVINGS

½ cup (1 stick) butter or margarine, melted

1¼ cups granulated sugar

1 teaspoon vanilla extract

2 eggs

⅔ cup all-purpose flour

½ cup HERSHEY'S Cocoa

¼ teaspoon baking powder

¼ teaspoon salt

1 package (8 ounces) cream cheese, softened

1 cup powdered sugar

½ cup chilled whipping cream

1¾ cups (10-ounce package) HERSHEY'S MINI KISSES BRAND Milk Chocolates

1 can (21 ounces) cherry pie filling, chilled

1 Heat oven to 350°F. Grease bottom only of 9-inch springform pan, or line 9-inch round cake pan with foil; grease bottom of foil.

2 Stir together melted butter, granulated sugar and vanilla in large bowl. Add eggs; using spoon, beat well. Stir together flour, cocoa, baking powder and salt; gradually add to egg mixture, beating with spoon until well blended. Spread batter in prepared pan.

3 Bake 25 to 30 minutes or until cake is set. (Cake will be fudgey and will not test done.) Remove from oven; cool completely in pan on wire rack.

4 Beat cream cheese and powdered sugar in medium bowl until well blended. Beat cream until stiff; gradually fold into cream cheese mixture, blending well. Spread over top of torte; refrigerate several hours or until set. With knife, loosen cake from side of pan; remove side of pan. (Or lift torte out of pan using foil; remove foil.)

5 Just before serving, place chocolates in 6-inch-wide heart outline in center of cake. Fill heart shape with cherries from pie filling; place chocolates all around outside edge. Serve cold, cut into wedges, with remaining pie filling. Cover; refrigerate leftover dessert.

Cherry Cordial Crème Cheesecake: Substitute HERSHEY'S KISSES BRAND Milk Chocolates filled with Cherry Cordial Crème, unwrapped, for the HERSHEY'S MINI KISSES BRAND Milk Chocolates.

Holiday Fudge Torte

- **1** cup all-purpose flour
- **¾** cup sugar
- **¼** cup **HERSHEY'S Cocoa**
- **1½** teaspoons powdered instant coffee
- **¾** teaspoon baking soda
- **¼** teaspoon salt
- **½** cup (**1 stick**) butter or margarine, softened
- **¾** cup dairy sour cream
- **1** egg
- **½** teaspoon vanilla extract
- **FUDGE NUT GLAZE** (recipe follows)

1 Heat oven to 350°F. Grease 9-inch round baking pan; line bottom with wax paper. Grease paper; flour paper and pan.

2 Stir together flour, sugar, cocoa, instant coffee, baking soda and salt in large bowl. Add butter, sour cream, egg and vanilla; beat on low speed of mixer until blended. Increase speed to medium; beat 3 minutes. Pour batter into prepared pan.

3 Bake 30 to 35 minutes or until wooden pick inserted in center comes out clean. Cool 10 minutes. Remove from pan to wire rack; gently peel off wax paper. Cool completely.

4 Prepare FUDGE NUT GLAZE.

5 Place cake on serving plate; pour glaze evenly over cake, allowing some to run down sides. Refrigerate until glaze is firm, about 1 hour. Cover; refrigerate leftover torte.

Fudge Nut Glaze

- **½** cup whipping cream
- **¼** cup sugar
- **1** tablespoon butter
- **1½** teaspoons light corn syrup
- **⅓** cup **HERSHEY'S SPECIAL DARK** Chocolate Chips or **HERSHEY'S** Semi-Sweet Chocolate Chips
- **¾** cup chopped **MAUNA LOA** Macadamia Nuts, hazelnuts or pecans
- **½** teaspoon vanilla extract

1 Combine all ingredients except nuts and vanilla in small saucepan. Cook over medium heat, stirring constantly, until mixture boils. Cook, stirring constantly, 5 minutes. Remove from heat.

2 Cool 10 minutes; stir in nuts and vanilla.

no-bake desserts

Chocolate Fried Ice Cream

MAKES 6 SERVINGS

1 quart vanilla ice cream

1 cup vanilla wafer crumbs (about 30 wafers, crushed)

½ cup finely chopped pecans

½ cup **MOUNDS Sweetened Coconut Flakes**

3 tablespoons **HERSHEY'S Cocoa**

2 eggs

Vegetable oil

CHOCOLATE NUT SAUCE (recipe follows)

1 Cover tray with wax paper. Form six ice cream balls with scoop; place on prepared tray. Cover; freeze several hours or until very firm.

2 Stir together vanilla wafer crumbs, nuts, coconut and cocoa in medium bowl; set aside. Beat eggs in small bowl. Coat ice cream balls with crumb mixture, pressing crumbs firmly into ice cream. Dip balls in beaten egg; coat again with crumb mixture. Place on prepared tray; freeze 2 hours or until very firm.

3 Just before serving, heat 2 inches oil in fry pan or deep fryer to 375°F. Remove 2 balls at a time from freezer; fry in hot oil 20 to 25 seconds or until browned. Drain; serve immediately with CHOCOLATE NUT SAUCE.

Chocolate Nut Sauce

3 tablespoons butter or margarine

⅓ cup pecan pieces

⅔ cup sugar

¼ cup **HERSHEY'S Cocoa**

⅛ teaspoon salt

½ cup light cream

½ teaspoon vanilla extract

1 Melt butter in small saucepan over low heat; add nuts. Cook and stir until lightly browned. Remove from heat; stir in sugar, cocoa and salt. Stir in light cream.

2 Cook over low heat, stirring constantly, until mixture just begins to boil. Remove from heat; stir in vanilla. Serve warm.

MAKES ABOUT 1 CUP SAUCE

Easy Chocoberry Cream Dessert

MAKES 10 TO 12 SERVINGS

2 packages (3 ounces each) ladyfingers, split

1 package (10 ounces) frozen strawberries in syrup, thawed and drained

2 envelopes unflavored gelatin

2 cups milk, divided

1 cup sugar

⅓ cup HERSHEY'S Cocoa or HERSHEY'S SPECIAL DARK Cocoa

¼ cup (½ stick) butter or margarine

1 teaspoon vanilla extract

2 cups frozen non-dairy whipped topping, thawed

Additional whipped topping (optional)

Fresh strawberries (optional)

Mint leaves (optional)

1 Place ladyfingers, cut side in, on bottom and around sides of 9-inch springform pan.

2 Purée strawberries in food processor. Sprinkle gelatin over 1 cup milk in medium saucepan; let stand 2 minutes to soften. Add sugar, cocoa and butter. Cook over medium heat, stirring constantly, until mixture is hot and gelatin is completely dissolved. Remove from heat; stir in remaining 1 cup milk, vanilla and puréed strawberries. Refrigerate until mixture begins to thicken.

3 Fold 2 cups whipped topping into gelatin mixture. Pour mixture into prepared pan. Cover; refrigerate until mixture is firm. Just before serving, remove side of pan. Garnish with additional whipped topping, fresh strawberries and mint, if desired. Cover; refrigerate leftover dessert.

Fudge Bottomed Chocolate Layer Pie

MAKES 6 TO 8 SERVINGS

1   cup **HERSHEY'S SPECIAL DARK Chocolate Chips, divided**

2   **tablespoons plus ¼ cup milk, divided**

1   **packaged chocolate crumb crust (6 ounces)**

1½   **cups miniature marshmallows**

1   **container (8 ounces) frozen non-dairy whipped topping, thawed and divided**

    Additional sweetened whipped cream or whipped topping (optional)

1 Place ⅓ cup chocolate chips and 2 tablespoons milk in microwave-safe bowl. Microwave 30 seconds at MEDIUM (50%); stir. If necessary, microwave an additional 15 seconds at a time, stirring after each heating, until chips are melted and mixture is smooth when stirred. Spread on bottom of crust. Refrigerate while preparing next step.

2 Place marshmallows, remaining ⅔ cup chocolate chips and remaining ¼ cup milk in small saucepan. Cook over medium heat, stirring constantly, until marshmallows are melted and mixture is well blended. Transfer to separate large bowl; cool completely.

3 Stir 2 cups whipped topping into cooled chocolate mixture; spread 2 cups mixture over chocolate in crust. Blend remaining whipped topping and remaining chocolate mixture; spread over surface of pie.

4 Cover; freeze several hours or until firm. Garnish as desired. Cover and freeze leftover pie.

Mini Chocolate Pies

1   package (4-serving size) vanilla cook & serve pudding and pie filling mix*

1   cup HERSHEY'S Mini Chips Semi-Sweet Chocolate

1   package (4 ounces) single-serve graham cracker crusts (6 crusts)

Whipped topping

Additional HERSHEY'S Mini Chips Semi-Sweet Chocolate, HERSHEY'S SPECIAL DARK Chocolate Chips or HERSHEY'S Semi-Sweet Chocolate Chips (optional)

Do not use instant pudding mix.

1 Prepare pudding and pie filling mix as directed on package; remove from heat. Immediately add 1 cup small chocolate chips; stir until melted. Cool 5 minutes, stirring occasionally.

2 Pour filling into crusts; press plastic wrap directly onto surface. Refrigerate several hours or until firm. Garnish with whipped topping and small chocolate chips.

Easy MINI KISSES Choco-Cherry Pie

MAKES ABOUT 8 SERVINGS

1	baked (9-inch) pie crust, cooled
1¾	cups (10-ounce package) HERSHEY'S MINI KISSESBRAND Milk Chocolates, divided
1½	cups miniature marshmallows
⅓	cup milk
1	cup (½ pint) cold whipping cream
1	can (21 ounces) cherry pie filling, chilled
	Whipped topping

1 Prepare pie crust.

2 Place 1 cup chocolate pieces, marshmallows and milk in medium microwave-safe bowl. Microwave at MEDIUM (50%) 1½ to 2 minutes or until chocolate is softened and mixture is melted and smooth when stirred; cool completely.

3 Beat whipping cream in small bowl until stiff; fold into chocolate mixture. Spoon into prepared crust. Cover; refrigerate 4 hours or until firm.

4 Garnish top of pie with cherry pie filling, whipped topping and remaining chocolates just before serving. Refrigerate leftover pie.

Crispy Chocolate Ice Cream Mud Pie

MAKES 8 SERVINGS

½   cup **HERSHEY'S Syrup**

⅓   cup **HERSHEY'S SPECIAL DARK** Chocolate Chips or **HERSHEY'S** Semi-Sweet Chocolate Chips

2   cups crisp rice cereal

4   cups (1 quart) vanilla ice cream, divided

4   cups (1 quart) chocolate ice cream, divided

Additional **HERSHEY'S** Syrup

1 Butter 9-inch pie plate.

2 Place ½ cup chocolate syrup and chocolate chips in medium microwave-safe bowl. Microwave at MEDIUM (50%) 45 seconds or until hot; stir until smooth. Reserve ¼ cup chocolate syrup mixture; set aside. Add cereal to remaining chocolate syrup mixture, stirring until well coated; cool slightly.

3 Press cereal mixture, using back of spoon, evenly on bottom and up side of prepared pie plate to form crust. Place in freezer 15 to 20 minutes or until crust is firm. Spread half of vanilla ice cream into crust; spoon reserved ¼ cup chocolate syrup mixture over layer. Spread half of chocolate ice cream over sauce.

4 Top with alternating scoops of vanilla and chocolate ice cream. Cover; return to freezer until serving time. Drizzle with additional chocolate syrup just before serving.

No-Bake Cherry Chocolate Shortcake

1 frozen loaf pound cake (10¾ ounces), thawed

1 can (21 ounces) cherry pie filling, chilled

⅓ cup HERSHEY'S Cocoa or HERSHEY'S SPECIAL DARK Cocoa

½ cup powdered sugar

1 container (8 ounces) frozen non-dairy whipped topping, thawed (3 cups)

1 Slice pound cake horizontally into three layers. Place bottom cake layer on serving plate; top with half of the pie filling, using mostly cherries. Repeat with middle cake layer and remaining pie filling; place rounded layer on top. Cover; refrigerate several hours.

2 Sift cocoa and powdered sugar onto whipped topping; stir until mixture is blended and smooth. Immediately spread over top and sides of cake, covering completely. Refrigerate leftover shortcake.

SPECIAL DARK Fudge Fondue

2   cups (12-ounce package) HERSHEY'S SPECIAL DARK Chocolate Chips

½   cup light cream

2   teaspoons vanilla extract

    Assorted fondue dippers such as marshmallows, cherries, grapes, mandarin orange segments, pineapple chunks, strawberries, slices of other fresh fruits, small pieces of cake or small brownies

1 Place chocolate chips and light cream in medium microwave-safe bowl. Microwave at MEDIUM (50%) 1 minute or just until chips are melted and mixture is smooth when stirred. Stir in vanilla.

2 Pour into fondue pot or chafing dish; serve warm with fondue dippers. If mixture thickens, stir in additional light cream, 1 tablespoon at a time. Refrigerate leftover fondue.

Stovetop Directions: Combine chocolate chips and light cream in heavy medium saucepan. Cook over low heat, stirring constantly, until chips are melted and mixture is hot. Stir in vanilla and continue as in Step 2.

PIES & DESSERTS

303

Refreshing Cocoa-Fruit Sherbet

MAKES 8 SERVINGS

1	ripe medium banana
1 ½	cups orange juice
1	cup (½ pint) half-and-half
½	cup sugar
¼	cup HERSHEY'S Cocoa

1 Slice banana into blender container. Add orange juice; cover and blend until smooth. Add remaining ingredients; cover and blend well. Pour into 8- or 9-inch square pan. Cover; freeze until hard around edges.

2 Spoon partially frozen mixture into blender container or large bowl. Cover; blend until smooth but not melted.

Pour into 1-quart mold. Cover; freeze until firm. Unmold onto cold plate and slice. Garnish as desired.

Variation: Add 2 teaspoons orange-flavored liqueur with orange juice.

Cocoa Cappuccino Mousse

- **1** can (**14 ounces**) **sweetened condensed milk (not evaporated milk)**
- **⅓** cup **HERSHEY'S Cocoa**
- **3** tablespoons butter or margarine
- **2** teaspoons powdered instant coffee or espresso, dissolved in 2 teaspoons hot water
- **2** cups (1 pint) cold whipping cream

1 Combine sweetened condensed milk, cocoa, butter and coffee in medium saucepan. Cook over low heat, stirring constantly, until butter melts and mixture is smooth. Remove from heat; cool.

2 Beat whipping cream in large bowl until stiff. Gradually fold chocolate mixture into whipped cream. Spoon into dessert dishes. Refrigerate until set, about 2 hours. Garnish as desired.

PIES & DESSERTS

St. Patrick's Day Parfaits

MAKES 6 SERVINGS

3   cups miniature or 30 large marshmallows

½   cup milk

2   tablespoons green crème de menthe*

1   cup HERSHEY'S SPECIAL DARK Chocolate Chips or HERSHEY'S Semi-Sweet Chocolate Chips

¼   cup powdered sugar

1½   cups heavy or whipping cream

*½ teaspoon mint extract plus 2 drops green food color can be substituted for the crème de menthe.

1 Combine marshmallows and milk in medium saucepan; cook over low heat, stirring constantly, until marshmallows are melted and mixture is smooth. Measure 1 cup marshmallow mixture into small bowl. Blend in crème de menthe; set aside. Add chocolate chips and powdered sugar to marshmallow mixture remaining in saucepan; return to low heat and stir until chips are melted. Remove from heat; cool to room temperature.

2 Whip cream just until soft peaks form; fold 1½ cups into marshmallow-mint mixture. Fold remaining whipped cream into chocolate mixture. Alternately spoon chocolate and mint mixtures into parfait glasses. Chill thoroughly or place in freezer until firm. Garnish as desired.

HERSHEY'S HUGS & KISSES
Pound Cake Torte

- **46**   **HERSHEY'S KISSES**BRAND **Milk Chocolates**
- **⅓**   **cup plus ½ cup whipping cream, divided**
- **2**   **teaspoons butter, softened**
- **½**   **teaspoon vanilla extract**
- **1**   **frozen loaf pound cake (10¾ ounces), partially thawed**
- **10**   **HERSHEY'S HUGS**BRAND **Candies**

1 Remove wrappers from chocolates. Combine chocolates and ⅓ cup whipping cream in small saucepan. Cook over low heat, stirring frequently, until smooth. Remove from heat. Stir in butter and vanilla until smooth; transfer to medium bowl. Refrigerate until firm enough to spread, about 1 hour.

2 Slice cake horizontally to make 3 layers. Arrange bottom layer on serving plate. Evenly spread ⅓ cup chocolate mixture over layer; top with second layer and spread with ⅓ cup mixture. Place remaining layer on top. Beat remaining ½ cup whipping cream until thickened; fold in remaining chocolate mixture. Refrigerate a few minutes if a more firm consistency is desired. Frost top, sides and ends of torte. Refrigerate about 6 hours. Remove wrappers from HERSHEY'S HUGSBRAND Candies. Garnish torte before serving. Cover; refrigerate leftover torte.

PIES & DESSERTS

Chocolate Nut Clusters

MAKES ABOUT 3 DOZEN CANDIES

1   cup HERSHEY'S SPECIAL DARK Chocolate Chips or HERSHEY'S Semi-Sweet Chocolate Chips

½   cup HERSHEY'S Premier White Chips

1   tablespoon shortening (do not use butter, margarine, spread or oil)

2¼   cups (11 ½-ounce package) lightly salted peanuts, divided

1 Place chocolate chips, white chips and shortening in small microwave-safe bowl. Microwave at MEDIUM (50%) 1 minute; stir. If necessary, microwave at MEDIUM an additional 15 seconds at a time, stirring after each heating, or until chips are melted and mixture is smooth when stirred. Reserve ¼ cup peanuts for garnish; stir remaining peanuts into chocolate mixture.

2 Drop by teaspoons into 1-inch candy cups; top each candy with a reserved peanut. Refrigerate, uncovered, until chocolate is set, about 1 hour. Store in airtight container in cool, dry place.

Peanut Butter Fondue

MAKES ABOUT 3 CUPS FONDUE

Selection of fruits and other fondue dippers

3⅓ cups (two 10-ounce packages) REESE'S Peanut Butter Chips

1½ cups light cream

1 Prepare ahead of time a selection of fresh fruit chunks for dipping: apples, bananas, pears, peaches, cherries, pineapple, oranges (brush fresh fruit with lemon juice to prevent browning). Cover; refrigerate until ready to serve. (Dried apples and apricots, marshmallows and bite-size pieces of pound cake can also be used for dipping.)

2 Place peanut butter chips and light cream in medium microwave-safe bowl. Microwave at MEDIUM (50%) 1½ minutes; stir. If necessary, microwave at MEDIUM an additional 30 seconds at a time, stirring after each heating, until chips are melted and mixture is smooth when stirred.

3 Pour into fondue pot; keep warm over low heat. Dip chunks of fruit into warm sauce with forks. Keep leftover sauce covered and refrigerated.

Note: Recipe may be halved using 1 package (10 ounces) REESE'S Peanut Butter Chips and ¾ cup light cream.

Chocolate Frozen Dessert

MAKES ABOUT 16 TO 18 SERVINGS

- ½ cup (1 stick) butter or margarine, melted
- 1 package (16 ounces) chocolate sandwich cookies, crushed (about 4 cups)
- ½ gallon vanilla ice cream (in rectangular block)
  CHOCOLATE SAUCE (recipe follows)
- ⅔ cup pecan pieces (optional)

1 Stir together butter and crushed cookies in medium bowl. Press mixture onto bottom of 13×9×2-inch pan or two 8-inch square pans.

2 Cut ice cream into 1-inch slices; place over crust, cutting slices to fit, if necessary. Cover; freeze 1 to 2 hours or until firm.

3 Uncover pan; spread CHOCOLATE SAUCE over ice cream. Sprinkle pecan pieces over top, if desired. Cover; freeze until firm.

Chocolate Sauce

- ½ cup (1 stick) butter or margarine
- 2 cups powdered sugar
- 1 can (12 ounces) evaporated milk
- 1 cup HERSHEY'S SPECIAL DARK Chocolate Chips or HERSHEY'S Semi-Sweet Chocolate Chips

1 Combine butter, powdered sugar, evaporated milk and chocolate chips in medium saucepan.

2 Cook over medium heat, stirring constantly, until mixture boils; boil and stir 8 minutes. Remove from heat; cool to room temperature (about 1 hour). Stir until smooth.

MAKES ABOUT 2½ CUPS SAUCE

Foolproof Dark Chocolate Fudge

3 cups (1½ packages, 12 ounces each) **HERSHEY'S SPECIAL DARK** Chocolate Chips or **HERSHEY'S** Semi-Sweet Chocolate Chips

1 can (14 ounces) sweetened condensed milk (not evaporated milk)

Dash salt

1 cup chopped walnuts

1½ teaspoons vanilla extract

1 Line 8- or 9-inch square pan with foil, extending foil over edges of pan.

2 Melt chocolate chips with sweetened condensed milk and salt in heavy saucepan over low heat. Remove from heat; stir in walnuts and vanilla. Spread evenly in prepared pan.

3 Refrigerate 2 hours or until firm. Remove from pan; place on cutting board. Peel off foil; cut into squares. Store loosely covered at room temperature.

Note: For best results, do not double this recipe.

index

Cookies

Cupcakes & Mini Cakes

Desserts

METRIC CONVERSION CHART

VOLUME MEASUREMENTS (dry)

1/8 teaspoon = 0.5 mL
1/4 teaspoon = 1 mL
1/2 teaspoon = 2 mL
3/4 teaspoon = 4 mL
1 teaspoon = 5 mL
1 tablespoon = 15 mL
2 tablespoons = 30 mL
1/4 cup = 60 mL
1/3 cup = 75 mL
1/2 cup = 125 mL
2/3 cup = 150 mL
3/4 cup = 175 mL
1 cup = 250 mL
2 cups = 1 pint = 500 mL
3 cups = 750 mL
4 cups = 1 quart = 1 L

VOLUME MEASUREMENTS (fluid)

1 fluid ounce (2 tablespoons) = 30 mL
4 fluid ounces (1/2 cup) = 125 mL
8 fluid ounces (1 cup) = 250 mL
12 fluid ounces (1 1/2 cups) = 375 mL
16 fluid ounces (2 cups) = 500 mL

WEIGHTS (mass)

1/2 ounce = 15 g
1 ounce = 30 g
3 ounces = 90 g
4 ounces = 120 g
8 ounces = 225 g
10 ounces = 285 g
12 ounces = 360 g
16 ounces = 1 pound = 450 g

DIMENSIONS

1/16 inch = 2 mm
1/8 inch = 3 mm
1/4 inch = 6 mm
1/2 inch = 1.5 cm
3/4 inch = 2 cm
1 inch = 2.5 cm

OVEN TEMPERATURES

250°F = 120°C
275°F = 140°C
300°F = 150°C
325°F = 160°C
350°F = 180°C
375°F = 190°C
400°F = 200°C
425°F = 220°C
450°F = 230°C

BAKING PAN SIZES

Utensil	Size in Inches/Quarts	Metric Volume	Size in Centimeters
Baking or Cake Pan (square or rectangular)	8×8×2	2 L	20×20×5
	9×9×2	2.5 L	23×23×5
	12×8×2	3 L	30×20×5
	13×9×2	3.5 L	33×23×5
Loaf Pan	8×4×3	1.5 L	20×10×7
	9×5×3	2 L	23×13×7
Round Layer Cake Pan	8×1½	1.2 L	20×4
	9×1½	1.5 L	23×4
Pie Plate	8×1¼	750 mL	20×3
	9×1¼	1 L	23×3
Baking Dish or Casserole	1 quart	1 L	—
	1½ quarts	1.5 L	—
	2 quarts	2 L	—